T0146611

DARK
GOLD

DARK GOLD

GOLD

THE
HUMAN SHADOW
AND THE
GLOBAL CRISIS

CAROLYNBAKER

iUniverse®

DARK GOLD
THE HUMAN SHADOW AND THE GLOBAL CRISIS

iUniverse books may be ordered through booksellers or by contacting:

iUniverse
1663 Liberty Drive
Bloomington, IN 47403
www.iuniverse.com
1-800-Authors (1-800-288-4677)

ISBN: 978-1-5320-3765-8 (sc)
ISBN: 978-1-5320-3764-1 (e)

Print information available on the last page.

iUniverse rev. date: 12/19/2017

Carolyn Baker reveals how we need to take responsibility for our disavowed personal shadows. Reclaiming our personal shadow projections is vital for countering the devastating impacts of the collective shadow. Baker invites us to dig deep and access the rich seam of "Dark Gold" that could inspire our collective transformative potential. This important book is a guide for deep healing in terms of how we treat ourselves and one another as well as other species and the natural world.
—*Dr. Mick Collins Lecturer, Retired Faculty of Medicine and Health Sciences, University of East Anglia, author of The Unselfish Spirit: Human Evolution in a Time of Global Crisis*

Carolyn Baker has done it again; she has taken a familiar topic and opened it with startling revelations. Her book is filled with wisdom, shining a light on the many ways the Shadow manifests in our culture. From war and racism, consumerism and New Age spirituality, Carolyn sees through our collective postures of superiority and invites us to do the hard work of redemption. At this critical time in our history, we urgently need her insights and guidance on how we may indeed uncover the Dark Gold that awaits us.
—*Francis Weller, author of The Wild Edge of Sorrow: Rituals of Renewal and the Sacred Work of Grief*

C. G. Jung wrote, "The future of mankind very much depends upon the recognition of the shadow." In her new book Dark Gold: The Human Shadow and the Global Crisis, Carolyn Baker masterfully

sheds light on the darkness of both the personal and collective aspects of the human shadow in a way that, I imagine, would truly give Jung hope for the future of humanity. To my mind, there is no more important work that any of us could do at the present moment in our history.
—*Paul Levy, author of Dispelling Wetiko: Breaking the Curse of Evil*

Once again Carolyn Baker invites us into a journey of self-reflection in the context of industrial civilization's collapse. But this time she plunges us even more deeply into the personal and collective shadow, where we hide what we don't want to notice or admit to as individuals, groups and nations. She shows that whether it's "othering" those not like us, or feeling entitled to privilege, the personal shadow writ large results in global war, injustice, and the current extinction of many species, including perhaps our own. She not only provides exercises for healing, she models the way forward. I was especially touched by her story of befriending a homeless man in her community. When she describes a day standing in his shoes, begging at an intersection, she vulnerably shares the myriad voices and emotions churning inside her. Don't miss it.
—*Janaia Donaldson, Producer, Peak Moment Television*

DEDICATION

For Buck and Betty and all people marginalized by the shadow illusion of separation.

Contents

Foreword

In Dark Gold, The Human Shadow and The Global Crisis, Carolyn Baker has courageously and generously provided the missing ingredient in much of our Sacred Activism by revealing the shadow as the treacherous saboteur of our desire to transform ourselves and the world. Compassionately but meticulously, she diagnoses the shadow's influence in both the individual psyche and collective consciousness and begs us to commit to a descent into shadow healing so that we can become wise students of our planetary predicament. In a time of anguish among all living beings, we cannot pursue a triumphalist approach to our activism, and Dark Gold reveals that nothing less than a rigorous understanding of the shadow and a humble willingness to confront it is necessary in the current dark night of the globe.

Carolyn Baker is not afraid to reveal elements of her own shadow and her ongoing journey of transformation forged by embracing, rather than rejecting, what the personal and collective shadow cry out to teach us. This book asks us to surrender to the power of heartbreak and the restructuring of the ego-based operating system so that we might discover the gold embedded in the shadow. It is a manual for reclaiming the apocalypse and immersing ourselves in limitless love and magnanimous service to the Earth community.

For me personally, Carolyn is not only a great friend but one of the essential spiritual teachers of our time, a pioneer of the highest integrity, who continues to amaze and instruct me and all those lucky enough to discover her work. Read this seminal, fierce, exquisitely written book and give it to everyone you know.

—Andrew Harvey, author of Radical Passion: Sacred Love and Wisdom In Action

INTRODUCTION

This thing of darkness, I acknowledge mine.
—William Shakespeare, The Tempest

Why would any author intending to sell books write one about the shadow? Why would anyone already aware of the unprecedented severity of the global crisis want to read a book on the shadow? Wouldn't this reader prefer the "catastrophe respite" of indulging in a book offering the hopeful consolation of radiant light and love?

Such questions arise from modernity's polarization of light and dark, love and adversity. In fact, this *is* a book of consolation, light, and love, but it does not lay out the culturally expected trajectory toward these values. The reader will not be able to grasp this, however, unless they are willing to dance with paradox—a reality with which the title, "Dark Gold" is replete.

The first concern that may arise is that this book has been written to shame the reader, perpetuating the notion that perhaps if one is sufficiently overwhelmed with guilt, one will realize the error of one's ways and shape up. After all, isn't that the Calvinistic American way? However, shame is not the response I desire. Rather, it's the cultivation of love, wholeness, and relatedness with all living beings, and when the shadow remains unexamined and unintegrated in the human psyche, these experiences are virtually impossible or at least hollow, muted, and significantly less vibrant than they might become with a more robust integration. James Hillman writes, "Loving oneself is no easy matter just because it means loving all of oneself, including the shadow where one is inferior and socially so unacceptable. The care one gives this humiliating part is also the cure."[1]

Carl Jung is said to have proclaimed on many occasions that the human shadow is 80 percent pure gold. In part, this is Jung's response to the Freudian perspective that humanity's dark side had absolutely no redeeming qualities. Conversely, Jung argued that rather than writing off our inner darkness as hopelessly irredeemable, we can choose to explore, excavate, and mine it because therein lie priceless riches of love and compassion. Or as Hillman would say, "… rotten garbage is also the fertilizer."[2]

But what *is* the human shadow? Joseph Campbell, mythologist and student of Jung states, "The Shadow is, so to say, the blind spot in your nature. It's that which you won't look at about yourself. This is the counterpart exactly of the Freudian unconscious, the repressed recollections as well at the repressed potentialities in you."[3]

In the following pages, we will closely examine both the personal shadow with which we all must contend individually, and the collective shadow to which the personal shadows of some seven billion people contribute. The influence of both on the human species is gargantuan, and the current global crisis that threatens to erase all life from planet Earth is a horrifying testimony to the destructiveness of the shadow unseen and unhealed.

This book offers options for embracing an alchemical odyssey that could alleviate the carnage and potentially transform the shadow of anyone willing to embark on the journey. With each passing conflagration of war, each ecological atrocity, each ethnic cleansing, each rape, pillage, and plunder of species and the planet, it seems less likely that the collective shadow will be healed, but if that transformation is possible, the only way to begin taking responsibility for the collective shadow is to be willing to be accountable for the personal one. Doing so may not transform *the* world, dear reader, but it may very well transform *your* world.

In *The Shadow In America: Reclaiming The Soul of a Nation*, Jacquelyn Small notes:

> *Until made conscious the shadow causes us to act in ways that create catastrophe or explosions of emotionalism. It stands there on the threshold of our unconscious mind, reflecting back to us our blind side. We must learn to embrace the shadow without trying to win it over. It is our teacher. We are often not able to hear the more kindly offerings of our friends, consequently, it must pop out from time to time to remind us from inside. When we try to deny the shadow, it multiplies. When instead, we choose to invite it in, we gain stability and expand consciousness, losing our self-righteousness, and becoming flexible, less defended, more balanced.*[4]

In her 2005 book *The Sacred Purpose of Being Human*, Small refers to the shadow as "...our holy grit. It's the sandpaper in your psyche that rubs you raw until you make it conscious."[5] Thus, the reader does not need the reminders of the shadow's presence and power presented in this book in order to be goaded, annoyed, discouraged, or flummoxed by it. On its own, the shadow relentlessly reminds us of its ubiquitous agenda. However, beyond providing information, this book offers specific practices and exercises for implementing deep shadow healing.

In my two previous books, *Love in the Age of Ecological Apocalypse: Cultivating the Relationships We Need to Thrive*, and *Collapsing Consciously: Transformative Truths for Turbulent Times,* I repeatedly emphasized the urgency of living lives of compassionate service to the planet. To that end, a number of tools were offered in both books. It is now incontrovertibly clear to me that without engaging with the personal and collective shadows in a process of conscious healing, the noble and necessary intention of compassionate service will be thwarted or perhaps even sabotaged by the machinations of unaddressed shadow material.

We commit to working with the shadow not only because failing to do so impedes our loftiest intentions, but because we are "prospectors" in search of the "dark gold." If there are precious metals to be mined, why would we settle for less? As Robert Johnson reminds us in *Owning Your Own Shadow*, "…these disowned parts are extremely valuable and cannot be disregarded. As promised of the living water, our shadow costs nothing and is immediately—and embarrassingly—ever present. To honor and accept one's own shadow is a profound spiritual discipline. It is whole-making and thus holy and the most important experience of a lifetime."[6]

In *Meeting the Shadow: The Hidden Power of the*

Dark Side of Human Nature, Connie Zweig and Jeremiah Abrams clarify six monumentally important reasons for transforming our relationship with the shadow, all of which are fundamental reasons for the writing of this book. Zweig and Abrams note, "A right relationship with the shadow offers us a great gift: to lead us back to our buried potentials."[7] Through *shadow-work*, the authors assert, we can:

- Experience more genuine self-acceptance, based on a more complete knowledge of who we are
- Defuse what we perceive as the negative emotions that erupt unexpectedly in our daily lives
- Feel less guilt and shame with respect to our so-called "negative" feelings and actions
- Recognize the projections that color our opinions of others and learn how to reclaim those projections
- Heal our relationships through honest self-examination and direct communication
- Access and use an untapped storehouse of creative energy through our dreams, artistic expression, and sacred ritual[8]

It must be noted, however, that when Zweig and Abrams edited their magnificent collection of articles by masters of Jungian psychology in the early 1990s, the global crisis had not reached its current magnitude of severity. At that point in human history, almost no one was discussing the possibility of near-term human extinction or the termination of life on Earth. While the anthology contains a number of articles addressing the collective shadow, what was not yet glaringly obvious was the extent to which humans were annihilating the planet.

Thus one gift of doing shadow work that may be added to Zweig and Abram's list is the potential for healing significant aspects of the Earth community. Since the collective shadow is comprised of the projections of individuals, even minimal reclamation of our own projections facilitates harmonious communication and interaction within the human community and the planet at large.

At the end of each chapter in this book, the reader will find specific suggested practices and exercises that support the reader in taking the material deeper and forging a more distinct path toward shadow healing. If one desires to mine the dark gold, these practices provide the working tools for launching and continuing the extraction of riches from the shadow. The suggested practices are also structured so that they might be employed not only by the individual reader but utilized by groups of "shadow prospectors" as well.

With the writing of each of my books, I become increasingly aware of all of the beings who make it possible to carry my voice and work forward. I am forever indebted to my friend and "soul brother" Andrew Harvey, whose wind is always at my back. I deeply appreciate my associations with Guy McPherson, Pauline Schneider, Kermit Heartsong, and Jill Angelo, as well as the tireless efforts of Peter Melton and Dean Walker in supporting my work.

I owe an eternal debt to Carl Jung, Meg Pierce, and all Jungian analysts and therapists worldwide who carry his work forward in a culture that cares little for his contribution to the healing of the human soul.

Thank you Janis, Judith, Daphne, and Kristen. Thank

you Sammy, for faithfully lying under my chair and inspiring me with the sounds of your dreams.

Thank you, dear reader, for picking up this book and daring to contemplate the journey of shadow healing.

Now, onward and inward.

> *An old Cherokee was teaching his grandson about life."A fight is going on inside me," he said to the boy." It is a terrible fight and it is between two wolves. One is evil – he is anger, envy, sorrow, regret, greed, arrogance, self-pity, guilt, resentment, inferiority, lies, false pride, superiority, and ego."*
>
> *"The other is good," the old man continued. "he is joy, peace, love, hope, serenity, humility, kindness, benevolence, empathy, generosity, truth, compassion, and faith. The same fight is going on inside you – and inside every other person, too."*
> *The grandson thought about it for a minute and then asked his grandfather."Which wolf will win?"*

You might have heard the story ends like this:

> *The old Cherokee simply replied, "The one you feed the most my son."*

In the Cherokee world, however, the story ends this way:

> *The old Cherokee simply replied, "If you feed them right, they both win."*

And the story goes on:

"You see, if I only choose to feed the good wolf, the bad one will be hiding around every corner waiting for me to become distracted or weak and jump to get the attention he craves. He will always be angry and always fighting the good wolf. But if I acknowledge him, he is happy and the good wolf is happy and we all win. For the bad wolf has many qualities – tenacity, courage, fearlessness, and strong-willedness – that I have need of at times and that the good wolf lacks. But the good wolf has compassion, caring, strength and the ability to recognize what is in the best interest of all.

"You see, son, the good wolf needs the bad wolf at his side. To feed only one would starve the other and they would become uncontrollable. To feed and care for both means they will serve you well and do nothing that is not a part of something greater, something good, something of life. Feed them both and there will be no more internal struggle for your attention. And when there is no battle inside, you can listen to the voices of deeper knowing that will guide you in choosing what is right in every circumstance. Peace, my son, is the Cherokee mission in life. A man or a woman who has peace inside has everything. A man or a woman who is pulled apart by the war inside him or her has nothing.

"How you choose to interact with the opposing forces within you will determine your life. Starve one or the other or guide them both."

THE PERSONAL

SHADOW

CHAPTER 1

WHAT IS THE HUMAN SHADOW?

Everyone carries a shadow, and the less it is embodied in the individual's conscious life, the blacker and denser it is. At all counts, it forms an unconscious snag, thwarting our most well-meant intentions

—C.G. Jung

The term "shadow," first introduced by Swiss psychiatrist Carl Jung, was a poetic as well as a psychological term. For Jung, the shadow was not a literal aspect of the mind or personality. Rather, it was the impulses, emotions, thoughts, and fantasies that humans banish from consciousness because they perceive them as unacceptable and incongruent with the image they wish to maintain in the world.

While we refer to the shadow as a noun, it is perhaps more accurate to understand that it is not some static energy lying dormant in the psyche. In fact, we may more precisely perceive the shadow as a verb—a very active aspect of the psyche that is busily engaged in concealing itself. Typically, it succeeds in doing so by way of the defense mechanism known as *projection*: an unconscious process by which we deny our own unacceptable qualities and ascribe them to other people.

Clinical and forensic psychologist and author Stephen Diamond states, that "The shadow is most destructive, insidious, and dangerous when habitually repressed and projected, manifesting in myriad psychological disturbances ranging from neurosis to psychosis, irrational interpersonal hostility, and even cataclysmic international clashes. Such deleterious symptoms, attitudes, and behavior stem from being possessed or driven by the dissociated yet undaunted shadow."[9]

In the article quoted above, Diamond uses "the shadow" and "the dark side" synonymously which I do not. This is because the shadow is not always "dark." The shadow is simply that which the individual says is "not me," which means that one can disavow positive qualities as well as negative ones. Moreover, it is quite possible to be aware of one's "dark side" and be familiar with one's socially unacceptable proclivities without banishing them to unconsciousness. For example, an impoverished individual may be conscious of the fact that when an armored bank truck is parked in front of the store he is entering, he wishes he could storm the vehicle, incapacitate the guards, and drive away with millions of dollars, when, in actuality he is simply entering the store to buy a sandwich. His dark side fantasy may roll around in his mind for days, but the obsession is not his shadow at work.

More dangerous and often deadly is the shadow material of which we are unconscious (or only scarcely conscious) that gets projected outward onto another person or group. A classic example is that of the member of a fundamentalist religion who teaches that same- gender relationships are immoral. The individual declares that he has never felt one second of attraction toward another male, and that such attraction is evil and unnatural. He insists that people choose same-gender relationships and that no one is born lesbian, gay, or bisexual, and he devotes enormous energy to castigating the LGBT community and attempting to "convert" LGBT people to a heterosexual lifestyle. In this typical scenario, same-gender attraction is clearly an aspect of the shadow that is being projected externally, as the individual demonizes a group that acts out his proclivities.

From time to time, my assertion is validated by former anti-gay spokespersons that later in their lives come out as gay. For example, in 2011, ex-gay ministry leader John Smid, former Executive Director of Love In Action Ministries, acknowledged his own homosexuality and apologized to lesbians and gays for attempting to shame them into rejecting their sexual orientation.[10] Additionally, in 2014, another former ex-gay leader, Christian Schizzel, denounced his former perspective and apologized to the LGBT community for leading its members to believe that a "cure" for homosexuality exists.[11] Homophobia is but one example of shadow projection—as are racism, misogyny, and contempt for the disabled and the homeless.

For Carl Jung, the choice to project the shadow, as opposed to examing it was a moral issue. Operating in the milieu of World War I and beyond, Jung wrote extensively about the price humanity pays for disowned, projected shadow material. In the 1985 documentary on Jung's life, "A Matter of The Heart," Jung sounds an even louder alarm with regard to the human shadow and the proliferation of nuclear weapons. He asserted,"The world hangs on a thin thread, and that is the psyche of man. Nowadays we are not threatened by elementary catastrophes. There is no such thing in nature as an H- bomb; that is all man's doing. We are the great danger. The psyche is the great danger."[12]

Additionally, Stephen Diamond writes:

> *Authentic spirituality requires consciously accepting and relating properly to the shadow as opposed to repressing, projecting, acting out and remaining naively unconscious of its repudiated, denied, disavowed contents, a sort of precarious pseudo-spirituality. "Bringing the shadow to consciousness," writes another of Jung's followers, Liliane Frey-Rohn (1967), "is a psychological problem of the highest moral significance. It demands that the individual hold himself accountable not only for what happens to him, but also for what he projects...Without the conscious inclusion of the shadow in daily life there cannot be a positive relationship to other people, or to the creative sources in the soul; there cannot be an individual relationship to the Divine."*[13]

Poet Robert Bly speaks of the shadow as a large bag we drag behind us for an entire lifetime into which we stuff aspects of ourselves that we choose not to own. Likewise, he asserts that each town or community or country has its own bag. Thus the shadow is not only personal and unique for each individual, but every individual is influenced by a collective shadow carried by the community at large.

Bly also emphasizes that our psyches are "natural projection machines" which thrust the shadow outward.

However, projection is not entirely undesirable because often, we cannot know our shadow without observing (or in some instances being blind-sided by) our projections. "The issue is not so much that we project," says Bly, "but how long we keep the projections out there."[14]

As stated above, the shadow is not always "dark." Jung and others spoke of a "bright shadow"—qualities that an individual disowns which are actually laudable. A man who disowns the feminine aspects of his psyche will project it onto a woman, as many men do with female partners and countless men have done throughout history with female icons such as Marilyn Monroe. Likewise, women who, as a result of their socialization, disown their personal power, may consciously or unconsciously seek a male partner who will take care of them financially and emotionally. When individuals can reclaim the bright shadow, they become more expansive, more empowered, whole human beings. Moreover, many people report that as a result of consciously doing shadow work, they discover a creative aspect of themselves that they previously did not realize existed or which they only rarely expressed. Suddenly that individual feels a deep desire to paint, play music, garden, or write poetry.

Maintaining the shadow also requires precious psychic energy. As Robert Bly notes, "When we have put a lot in our private bag, we often have as a result little energy. The bigger the bag, the less energy."[15] One inestimable benefit of shadow healing work is the restoration of psychic energy previously unavailable to us.

Psychotherapy offers one avenue for bringing the shadow to consciousness and assimilating it, but other options exist as well. Some of the tools available will be offered in this book because in current times, psychotherapy, particularly that which provides deep shadow exploration, is becoming increasingly inaccessible. From my perspective, anything we can do, any tools we can implement which assist us in making the shadow conscious and integrating it in the psyche, should be utilized. At the same time, it is crucially important to understand that shadow work should not be undertaken in isolation or without support from trusted others.

In addition to the personal shadow we each carry, Jung wrote extensively about the collective shadow. Poet and author Megge Fitz-Randolph explains:

> *According to Carl Jung there are two types of shadow projection: the personal and the collective. The personal shadow is a projection of the individual's unconscious and unlived life onto another individual. The collective shadow is a projection of the collective unconscious onto another group. Similarly, the projection may arise from one whole group onto another group. This is how entire populations of people are made into enemies. This is also what props up racial, religious, and ethnic suspicion and hatred. Whenever one feels oneself or one's group superior to another, one is engaged in shadow projection. This 'other' becomes the scapegoat to carry away the sins of the father. The so-called sins are never carried away. They just go underground where*

*they breed more hatred and shadow material. It
sets up a vicious cycle.*[16]

It is imperative that we accept the existence of the
shadow both personal and collective and consciously explore
and integrate the material we find there. In doing so, we
reclaim the unprecedented wholeness that has been eclipsed
by our efforts to maintain the shadow. The rewards in doing
so are incalculable.

In an interview entitled "How Dark is the Shadow?"
Andrew Harvey states that if we stand calmly in the depth
of our divine consciousness, we will find strength to really
look at the shadow and make it conscious, particularly in the
context of the global crisis. Making the shadow conscious,
Jung said, is the way to enlightenment. While Harvey
explains the difference between the personal and collective
shadows, he also emphasizes that the two shadows collude
with each other influencing us individually and collectively.
Harvey notes that the collective shadow, which psychically
affects all human beings, has five specific categories of
which we must be aware.

- Disbelief—Not being able to believe that something
  so enormous and horrific as the global crisis with all
  of its dreadful features could be happening.
- Denial—When the shadow of disbelief is uncovered,
  denial emerges. Our terror of what is happening
  and our determination to prevent the inevitable
  consequences of the crisis compel us to deny the
  obvious.
- Dread—Beneath disbelief and denial is the
  terrifying dread of the heartbreak and suffering

toward which all living beings on this planet are currently catapulting.

- Disillusion—When our disbelief, denial, and dread are penetrated, we invariably encounter disillusion with ourselves and all of humanity; this is attended by molten rage. This rage is particularly terrifying because we realize that despite all of the messengers and allies that have attempted to change the course of our actions, the human species has chosen a disastrous addiction to power and greed, which are now confronting the entire planet with an unimaginable ordeal.

- Death Wish—Lying beneath disbelief, denial, dread, and disillusion is a death wish—a desire not to be here at all in an era that demands so much of all of us.

Can we alter the course of this downward spiral of the personal and collective shadows? Indeed we can, and this involves conscious shadow work, perhaps using some of the wide assortment of tools offered in this book. These are best facilitated in conjunction with deep meditation or some regular spiritual practice as well as our connections with supportive friends.

The personal shadow, colluding with the "Five D's" above, must be addressed because it prevents us from being fully present to heal the collective shadow's miasma. Harvey highlights five aspects of the personal shadow:

- Narcissism—Our preoccupation with ourselves is an epidemic and prevents us from genuine concern about what is happening around us. Unless our narcissism is tempered, we cannot possibly rise to meet this crisis of epic proportions with grace.

- Terror of Taking a Stand—We are all afraid of acknowledging what we really know because the kind of demonization we receive from speaking the truth causes us to shrink from doing so.
- The Love of Comfort—We are addicted to a lifestyle that we are willing to perpetuate even when it is obvious that the world is being destroyed by it. Thus we are unwilling to alter our living arrangements or venture into service in the world that would require our taking risks or moving beyond our comfort zone.
- Woundology—Rooted in narcissism, this perspective assumes that we cannot act in the world or do deep shadow work until we have healed all or most of our childhood traumas. Moreover, our private inventory of wounding prevents us from perceiving the reality that millions of beings around the world are suffering far more than we ever have or ever will. But, Harvey emphasizes, we will never be able to heal our wounds until we make a commitment to serve the healing of others.
- The Golden Shadow—The adoration of other activists, healers, or celebrities. We allow these people to take action for us because we are afraid to do it ourselves. The illusion is that if we adore this person whom we admire, we are really doing the work that needs to be done. Rather, this is a projection, albeit a positive one, that needs to be reclaimed. (The dynamics of projection and

reclaiming projection will be examined in Chapter 12.) What we adore in others are qualities that are crying out to be developed within ourselves.

The subsequent chapters in this book offer a deeper perspective on these five collective and five personal shadow aspects, and offer a variety of exercises and practices for transforming them. The journey of shadow transformation may be long and rigorous, and along the way we require inspiration and encouragement such as we find in these words from Joseph Campbell's *Reflections on The Art of Living*:

> *The dark night of the soul comes just before revelation. When everything is lost, and all seems darkness, then comes the new life and all that is needed.*

— — — — — — — — — — —

SUGGESTED PRACTICE: To be certain that the reader has an overall grasp of the shadow, throughout the book I will offer specific exercises throughout the book that the reader can apply personally, and will hopefully invite him/her to embark on a journey of shadow healing. Here at the end of Chapter 1, I refer the reader to the work of Peter and Nicole Shepherd at http://www.trans4mind. com/jamesharveystout/shadow.htm who offer 10 practical exercises for discerning the personal shadow along with 8 techniques for beginning shadow healing. These involve journaling practices, observations of one's behavior, dream work, and tracking the interaction of these over a specific time period, for example 2-3 months.

CHAPTER 2

IT'S ALL ABOUT POWER

VICTIM, TYRANT, REBEL, SAVIOR

In this process of self-discovery, you have to account for all the missing pieces of yourself, even those you labeled negative. You can no longer choose to ignore these missing parts by creating a shadow over them. You must make another plan for the negative that does not involve suppression, avoidance, or denial.

—Leslie Temple Thurston, Marriage of Spirit

When we embrace all that we are, even the evil, the evil in us is transformed.

—Andrew Bard Schmookler

…the cure of the shadow is a problem of love. How far can our love extend to the broken and ruined parts of ourselves, the disgusting and perverse?

—James Hillman

In her 2000 book, *Marriage of Spirit: Enlightened Living In Today's World*, Leslie Temple Thurston offers a comprehensive toolkit for working consciously with the shadow. While the term "marriage of spirit" may sound esoteric, it simply means "making the unconscious conscious, bringing the shadow into light, and marrying spirit with matter. It's about becoming conscious of the luminous core of enlightenment that is within each of us."[17] Moreover, "enlightenment" is not a condition or evolutionary stage, but rather an aspect of aliveness within each human being that we brought to this planet and which we can never lose.

In a broken, wounded, and very non-enlightened world, and particularly within industrial civilization, human relationships are constructed around power. We see the dynamics of power played out daily and sometimes moment to moment in the arenas of money, sex, relationships, jobs, survival, and more. Fundamentally, we conduct our power relationships by assuming four specific roles: *Victim, Tyrant, Rebel, and Savior.*

The *tyrant* is the one who is in the position of power and control, often has the authority, and is usually held in a negative light. The *savior* is also in a position of power, but is held in a positive light. The *victim* appears to be powerless, not in control and subservient, and usually seems weak and helpless on the surface. The *rebel* also appears not to have power, reacts to this, and says *no* to the authority.

It is extremely important to understand that these roles are not fixed. As we find ourselves caught up in them, if we pay closer attention, we will also discover that we are moving in and out of the four different roles from time to time—or perhaps daily or even hourly. The veils between them are extremely thin, and people change roles so quickly that they don't even realize what is happening.

In *Marriage of Spirit*, Leslie Temple Thurston takes a closer look at these power dynamics:

> *For example, let's look at the tyrant-victim-rebel dynamic. You may have an outside situation or person that you feel tyrannizes you in some way. Perhaps it is a boss or a coworker or a parent.*
>
> *From the level of duality, you have two choices. You can either feel like a victim or choose to play the rebel. Say for example you play the victim. You may feel it would be rude or improper or too scary to express your anger at the tyrant, so you keep it in; you feel victimized and abused. You may feel sorry for yourself on the one hand, feeling helpless, powerless, subservient and not in control. You may even revel in it for a while, gaining sympathy or attention from friends, which feels good. But on the other hand, you have suppressed your anger, and so you have this seething rage under the surface at the other person. You rebel against the authority inwardly, feeling self-righteous and indignant perhaps, trying to regain some measure of control of the situation, even if it is not an outer form of control. It is a way of feeling some degree of power, albeit inwardly. Maybe you just harbor resentment, a lesser degree of anger but still a form of inner rebellion. So, on the surface, you appear as a victim, but covertly, you are a rebel. Your rebellious, unexpressed response is still an attack, though. You are an inner tyrant! Your thoughts and feelings have an enormous impact on other people around you, especially those they are projected at, even though they are unseen with*

physical eyes. We can even make others sick with our unexpressed projections. So, your rebelling has flowed right into tyrannizing. The person who tyrannized you is now your victim, even though the person may not know it consciously.

Maybe you do occasionally blow up and choose to express yourself at your petty tyrant, reacting, letting emotions fly, having your voice. You are choosing to rebel against the authority, saying, "I will not be victimized by this person! I will show them! I have power too!" So, you rebel outwardly and try to take some form of control of the situation, maybe making you feel a little better, making you feel like the powerful one. Then, you become the authority or the tyrant outwardly, and the other person becomes your victim. The cycle repeats itself ad infinitum in the realm of egoic power dynamics. It is a win-lose every time.

The savior character is also a form of being in power or control. Some people idealize the authority in their lives, making the authority a savior or rescuer. The situation can become unbalanced then and flip into its opposite, in which case the idealizing becomes demonizing, tearing the authority off the pedestal, turning the authority into either a tyrant or a victim or both. This kind of scenario repeats itself again and again; it continually cycles.

Sometimes people cherish their roles as saviors. Taking care of others can be a beautiful thing. However, when it is done from the level of ego, not from a clear place, not with healthy boundaries, perhaps done with the desire to get something back (approval or other rewards), or done in a codependent or manipulative way, it becomes unbalanced. The nature of duality is that everything in time turns into its opposite. So, the would-be saviors can count on eventually making those they take care of feel like needy, helpless victims who feel resentful or angry. This, of course, puts the savior into the role of the tyrant.

No matter how much you try on the different costumes of tyrant-savior-victim-rebel, you don't find lasting happiness[18]

It is important to understand the term "ego" as used in this excerpt from *Marriage of Spirit.* The ego, as defined here the same way it is defined by Jung: is that part of the psyche that serves as a gatekeeper between the conscious and unconscious minds.

The ego is absolutely necessary in order to function in the world. At the same time, it is the custodian of one's self-image and is almost always invested in looking competent and in charge. Jungian analyst Edward Whitmont wrote, "In order to protect its own control and sovereignty, the ego instinctively puts up a great resistance to the confrontation with the shadow; when it catches a glimpse of the shadow, the ego most often reacts with an attempt to eliminate it."[19]

While the ego is a necessary and desirable aspect of the psyche, it becomes distorted, particularly as we are socialized to become compliant members of industrial civilization, and it increasingly obscures the enlightened inner core. Shadow healing by definition demands a commitment—to bring the shadow to consciousness in spite of the ego's machinations. In the process, the ego will resist mightily, but if we persevere, ultimately it will be humbled and will assume a more appropriate place in the psyche, as opposed to being its dominating force.

Jungian analyst John Sanford reminds us that Jung believed 90 percent of the shadow is pure gold. "Whatever has been repressed holds a tremendous amount of energy, with a great positive potential. So the shadow, no matter how troublesome it may be, is not intrinsically evil. The ego, in its refusal of insight and its refusal to accept the entire personality, contributes much more to evil than the shadow."[20]

Thurston's *Marriage of Spirit* offers an invaluable toolkit for transforming the *victim, tyrant, rebel, savior* dynamic. Additionally, these same tools can be applied on a larger scale to the collective shadow, and utilizing them, we can perceive incisively the power dynamics in local, regional, and international relations. While the *victim, tyrant, rebel, savior* dynamic does not encompass every aspect of the shadow and its activity, it is a splendid beginning for launching the journey of shadow healing.

Additional tools such as meditation, art, and ritual can be extremely useful; however, it is important to understand that spiritual practice itself can stir the shadow. In "Meeting The Dark Side In Spiritual Practice," William Carl Eichman offers the caveat: "If you undertake spiritual practice, you will be confronted by your dark side. This is an axiom. The spiritual quest is dangerous, just as the books say. Seeking truth means experiencing pain and darkness, as well as clear white light."[21]

Creative expression can be supremely useful in containing disturbing images and emotions that may arise during shadow healing work. Likewise, both dream work and the skillful use of Earth-based ritual can both contain an excess flow of psychic energy assisting us in viewing shadow material in proper perspective.

The definition of "power" we have embraced as a result of our enculturation in an industrial growth society serves only to destroy us and the Earth community. When we are willing to mine the dark gold of the personal shadow, our definition of power is transformed by love. When we can come to love what the ego considers the worst in us, we become mercifully and skillfully equipped to love what appears unlovable and intolerable in our world. When we are willing to fall to the bottom of the abyss, there we find, in Joseph Campbell's words, "the voice of salvation."[22] Consciously engaging the shadow for the purpose of transforming it will unequivocally catapult us to the bottom of the abyss. And, says Campbell, "The black moment is the moment when the real message of transformation is going to come. At the darkest moment comes the light."[23]

To reiterate, the shadow is a personal and collective moral issue. Every human being is responsible for their personal shadow. Much of this book will focus on the collective shadow, but this cannot be transformed unless individuals are willing to explore and heal their personal shadow dynamics. Otherwise, individuals will persist in projecting their inner worlds onto the outer world, until human beings seal the extinction of the planet and their own species. This may have already occurred; it may be too late for all living beings on earth; but even if that is so, how do we wish to live the remainder of our days? Will you, dear reader, choose to drag behind you the long, black bag of unexplored shadow material, insisting that all of our planet's ills are the fault of the other, or will you opt to mine the dark gold of the personal shadow in order to minimize the projections that are presently annihilating life on Earth?

I offer no illusions about the difficulty of the mining. It requires a descent into dark, terrifying depths that place you squarely in what may feel like the black maw of death. And that is precisely where you will discover the gold—the gold you came here to mine. In fact, your soul will never allow you to settle for less.

More than seven centuries ago, a man who knew both the agonizing and glorious territories of the journey better than most, the mystical poet Rumi, exquisitely depicted the risks and the rewards in the following poem.

> *The grapes of my body can only become wine*
> *After the winemaker tramples me.*
>
> *I surrender my spirit like grapes to his trampling*
> *So my inmost heart can blaze and dance with joy.*
>
> *Although the grapes go on weeping blood and*
> *sobbing "I cannot bear any more anguish, any*
> *more cruelty"*
>
> *The trampler stuffs cotton in his ears: "I am not*
> *working in ignorance*
>
> *You can deny me if you want, you have every*
> *excuse, But it is I who am the Master of this Work.*

And when, through my Passion, you reach perfection, You will never be done praising my name.[24]

— — — — — — — — — — —

SUGGESTED EXERCISE: In this chapter I have explained the Victim/Tyrant/Rebel/Savior dynamic. More valuable than merely reading about it is applying an exercise recommended in Leslie Temple Thurston's *Marriage of Spirit,* which can also be found in the Appendix of this book. In the exercise, you will explore this four-part power dynamic by focusing on one role and tracking how it interfaces with the other three. Eventually, the practice takes you into all four roles. This compelling process gently but powerfully facilitates not only heightened awareness of how we become ensnared in the dynamic, but also how to prevent and heal this shadow cycle of harm and disempowerment.

> *Alchemists in the Middle Ages were intent on discovering the philosopher's stone, a legendary substance that could turn iron into gold. Their efforts mirror the timeless attempt of humans to control life rather than face it, by turning what we don't like into something else. In truth, the gold of life waits in the iron and in the difficulty, no matter its shape. Everything is inherently of great value and we don't have to turn any one thing into anything else. Rather, we need to discover the gold already there. More to the point, we're asked to pan for the gold in our suffering; to sift through the truth of our feelings in order to discover the many forms of gold dust that every experience carries.*

When we resist both things as they are and how we feel about what is, we pour our efforts into turning things into gold, a misperception that can occupy our energy and worth for years. When we can face what we're given and feel our feelings all the way through, we find the value—the gold— in everything and in ourselves. Then we're close to discovering the meaning imbedded in life...

Often our attempt to turn what we don't like or fear into something else has us bypass the very lessons put in our path to break our self- centeredness. Often, our attempt to turn our suffering into something shiny and distracting has us skip over the pain waiting to transform us, as we try to paint every difficulty as rosy and promising. When we are afraid of what we feel, turning one thing into another removes us from what we have to face in order to truly live.

—Mark Nepo, Endless Practice: BecomingWhoYouWere Born To Be

THE COLLECTIVE
SHADOW

CHAPTER 3

THAT'S NOT WHO WE ARE

THE SHADOW OF TORTURE

> *If only it were so simple! If only there were evil people somewhere insidiously committing evil deeds, and it were necessary only to separate them from the rest of us and destroy them. But the line dividing good and evil cuts through the heart of every human being. And who is willing to destroy a piece of his own heart?*
> **—Alexander Solzhenitsyn, The Gulag Archipelago**

In December 2014, the United States Senate Intelligence Committee released a report on torture by the Central Intelligence Agency in regard to the September 11, 2001 attacks and the subsequent wars in Afghanistan and Iraq. Four months prior to the release of the report, President Barack Obama stated in a press conference, "We tortured some folks," then moved on to other topics after emphasizing "that's not who we are". The December report, however, exposed the gory details of what "we tortured some folks" actually meant.

Equally as heinous as the crimes committed against human beings by American torturers was the role American psychologists played in managing the torture. In a Marketwatch story titled "Two psychologists earned $81 million from CIA torture program," and and another story "Weaponizing Psychology," we learned not only about the torture horrors devised by the psychologists, but collusion in the torture program by the American Psychological Association.[25] [26]

That same month, journalist Charles Blow, asked the question in his New York Times piece, "America, Who Are we?"

> *Are we — or better yet, should we be — a nation that tortures detainees, or targets and kills American citizens with drones, or has broad discretion to spy on the American public? Should we be a country hamstrung over how to deal with millions of undocumented immigrants, or our gun violence epidemic, or our growing income inequality? Should we be a country that accepts bias in its criminal justice system, a country of mass incarceration and a country where so many young black men can be killed by the police? Who are we?*[27]

Paralleling the release of the torture report was an eruption of protests across the United States against the rampant murder of young black men by predominantly white police officers—an issue we shall return to in Chapter 4 of this book. At the moment, I wish to focus on the statements made by Barack Obama at the time of the report's release. "No nation is perfect," Obama said, as well as, "We tortured some folks," and "That's not who we are." All three of these utterances are classic examples of America's shadow turning itself inside out to justify its disgraceful behavior.

One of the most successful maneuvers utilized by the shadow is "No one is perfect." From the shadow's perspective, this is supposed to absolve the guilty party and make everything mostly, if not entirely, OK. The intention is to hook the accuser's empathy and shame regarding their own transgressions.

When confronted with the hard evidence of America's involvement in torture, the President of the United States resorts to "no nation is perfect." Yet isn't it curious how when the foreign policy agenda of the United States is to initiate regime change, political assassination, or a coup d'etat in another country, the implicit assumption is that it can do so with impunity because it is, in fact, morally superior—a blameless nation founded on countless values that justify its aggression? With regard to the *victim, tyrant, savior, rebel* dynamic, in its early history the United States was the *victim* and then became a *rebel* in order to cast off a horrible *tyrant.* More than two centuries later, the United States has become the *savior,* purporting to bring "democracy" to millions of *victims* and quashing all who *rebel* against it. Ultimately, it has revealed itself as the world's richest and most powerful *tyrant.*

"We tortured some folks," was a public relations tactic devised four months prior to the release of the torture report to prepare the American public for the horrors the report would reveal— horrors that the Obama Administration hoped would be tempered by the President's downhome, folksy style. What the statement actually communicates is: "Yeah, we tortured some people, and that wasn't nice," immediately followed by, "But that's not who we are." In quintessential shadow- speak, Obama was fundamentally saying that we were a bit naughty, and we should hang our heads just slightly, but hey, that's not who we really are. But the shadow-speak doesn't end there. After stating "no nation is perfect," Obama asserted that "one of the strengths that makes America exceptional is our willingness to openly confront our past, face our imperfections, make changes and do better."[28]

So yes, we've behaved badly, but remember—we are exceptional because we take responsibility for our errors, learn from our mistakes, and change our course of action to one that is noble, virtuous, and exemplary.

Naturally, I am riveted by the word "exceptional" because it is so laden with implications. In shadow-speak, "exceptional" in this context means that America has the unique ability to learn from its errors. Unlike "those other nations," we are so virtuous that we immediately admit the error of our ways, and like St. Paul on the road to Damascus, allow ourselves to be blinded by the light, fall on our knees, and repent our sins. This, the shadow argues, is what makes us exceptional.

However, the word "exceptional" as pertaining to the United States has an entirely different meaning, when used in another context. The myth of American exceptionalism has persisted since Europeans landed on the shores of North America and began pillaging and plundering every person and object in their path. From the moment the Puritans asserted that the New World of America was a "New

Jerusalem," a "city set on a hill," a "light unto the world"—from that moment, American exceptionalism has been so deeply instilled in us that it often feels as if it were part of our DNA.

The shadow loves nothing more than the notion of exceptionalism. In fact, it thrives on it. Exceptionalism's twin, of course, is entitlement. We are entitled because we are exceptional. We are entitled internationally to extend the tentacles of corporate capitalism to every inch of the planet, and we are entitled intra-nationally by "virtue" of race, class, and economic status, to deliriously consume everything in sight and oppress and dominate all whom we deem not exceptional.

In his 2010 book *Madness At The Gates Of The City: The Myth Of American Innocence,* Barry Spector writes extensively of "Otherness" or "Othering"—defining ourselves by who we are *not*. For example, a white heterosexual male may define himself as *not* female, *not* Hispanic, and *not* gay. Othering inherently deems whoever we are *not* as inferior and justifies the oppression of "those people". Spector notes that Othering is most pronounced in monotheistic religions and that it can range from a mild sense of Othering, to an obsession about the Other as is ubiquitous in racist or homophobic groups that make the elimination of the Other their life's mission. Othering is an invariable outcome of exceptionalism and entitlement. One constructs one's identity out of the Othering process, in juxtaposition to the Other. That is to say, I am who I am because I am *not* you. In indigenous cultures, identity is formed in the opposite manner: I am who I am because you and I are not separate.

I cannot be who I am without knowing who you are. We interdependently need each other to complete our identity.

In this second decade of the twenty-first century as the paradigm and infrastructure of industrial civilization crumble around us, we are flailing to find our identity both individually and collectively. Charles Blow cries out, "Who are we?" This is a question with which every individual and every nation must periodically grapple. Failing to do so or attempting to answer the question with superficial, undiscerning responses is compost for the shadow.

As Socrates knew well, asking who one is or who a nation is, can be an excruciating endeavor. Ancient indigenous societies constructed elaborate rites of passages for their youth—initiatory experiences that were inherently painful. These cultures understood that only when an individual is confronted with an ordeal that constitutes a brush with death that he or she may not survive—only when that individual is compelled to go within and access the resources of their sacred core to sustain them in the ordeal—can they possibly discover who they are and what they came here to do.

A journalist asks a question that is written and received on an intellectual level. Let's all *think* about who we are. Yet, we can never arrive at the answers with the intellect. Only in the personal or collective initiatory experience do we have any hope of discovering our authentic identity. Part of who we are is that we have a shadow, and that shadow is ugly, brutal, and relentlessly Othering, and the more we scream, "but that's not who we are," the more intransigent the shadow becomes and the more righteously justified we feel in persevering in our madness.

For indigenous cultures, initiation is a singular event

that occurs in the life of a young person; it concludes with his or her surviving the ordeal and transitioning into adulthood in order to assume a specific role in the community. Yet beyond a literal ceremony, initiation itself is an archetype, a universal theme in human consciousness among countless other themes such as birth, death, marriage, the battle of good and evil, the scapegoat, the martyr, the lover, and more. While we may not directly engage with all archetypes, one that we cannot escape is initiation. While in modernity, few communities on earth provide literal, formal rites of passage for their young, life offers symbolic initiations or thresholds that frequently manifest through loss in one form or another. A divorce, a bankruptcy, the loss of a job, a house burned to the ground, the loss of a body part, a terminal diagnosis—all are initiations that catapult us to initiatory ground where like the indigenous youth enduring a life-threatening ordeal, we are dragged to the depths of the psyche. In what feels like abject wasteland, we can distract, deny, and resist further descent, or we can become a student of the ordeal, allowing it to transform, mature, wizen, and humble us.

The transformation of the human shadow is made possible by our willingness to submit to a rite of passage. We always have the choice not to do so, yet life is not easily dissuaded, and for many human beings, life appears to consist of one initiation after another. Conversely, some individuals, as well as nations, appear to move through life unscathed—always in charge, always in the game, always triumphant. Industrial civilization's paradigm molds us to revere conquest and despise failure. Initiation, descent, and the possibility of toppling from lofty heights of achievement are abhorrent, and when these rear their ugly heads, the shadow works overtime to thwart them.

All empires collapse. All species eventually go extinct. As global warming literally sears us in the fires of catastrophic climate change, we have been spiritually and emotionally thrust into the alchemical fires of planetary initiation now engulfing all nations, all humans, and all living beings. On the physical level, the purpose of ancient alchemy was the transmutation of baser metal into gold. Intrigued by the symbolic relationship between alchemy and psychological healing, during the last half of his life Jung framed the healing process as an alchemical one because on the psycho-spiritual level, alchemy is the transformation of consciousness. What could interfere with the process, of course, would be an unwillingness to enter the fire.

Planet Earth has entered the literal fires of abrupt climate change and the symbolic fires of endless war, economic meltdown, nuclear contamination, and the depletion of countless natural treasures which humans call "resources." We cannot escape the literal fires, but we have the option of resisting their alchemical significance. Conversely, we may choose to perceive our predicament as one that represents the most profound alchemical transformation in the history of our species. This will only be possible, however, if we cease repeating, "That's not who we are," and instead fall on our knees in heartbreak and remorse, crying out from the depths, "Who are we?!"

SUGGESTED PRACTICES:

1) Consciously and thoughtfully view the 1995 movie "Dead Man Walking." Carefully observe the contrast of the two characters: Sister Helen Prejean as portrayed by Susan Sarandon, and Matthew Poncelet as portrayed by Sean Penn. Allow yourself to absorb the monstrosity of the crime Poncelet committed; also, if possible, allow yourself to feel compassion for him as he faces execution. Likewise, feel your compassion for the families of his victims. In addition, pay close attention to the fear, vulnerability, uncertainty, and yet unflinching compassion of Sister Helen.

   After viewing the movie, journal your emotions and notice how the movie impacted you—even if you have seen it many times. What did you learn about "the other"? What did you notice in yourself throughout the movie? Notice and journal about the complexity of the situation. Be aware of the "Otherness" of the main characters: Poncelet is "the Other" for the families of his victims; Sister Helen is "the Other" for him. She is also "the Other" for Poncelet's victims' families. How is the "Othering" transformed for some of the characters?

2) Volunteer for some form of service in your community that involves interacting with those who are considered "the Other." This may include homeless people, incarcerated inmates,

developmentally disabled people, or outpatient mentally ill individuals. Notice the subtle and obvious ways you "Other" them and how you feel "Othered" by them. Notice your fear, disgust, heartbreak, and feelings of helplessness as you interact with them. Reflect deeply on the following questions: What helps you feel connected with these individuals? What helps them feel connected with you? What feels alienating for you and for them? In what ways do you identify with or resonate with them? Are there parts of you or your experience that are mirrored by these individuals? Journal your experiences and emotions carefully.

Chapter 4

American Apartheid

I CAN'T BREATHE—BLACK LIVES MATTER

Racism is both overt and covert. It takes two, closely related forms: individual whites acting against individual blacks, and acts by the total white community against the black community. We call these individual racism and institutional racism. The first consists of overt acts by individuals, which cause death, injury or the violent destruction of property. This type can be recorded by television cameras; it can frequently be observed in the process of commission. The second type is less overt, far more subtle, less identifiable in terms of specific individuals committing the acts. But it is no less destructive of human life. The second type originates in the operation of established and respected forces in the society, and thus receives far less public condemnation than the first type. When white terrorists bomb a black church and kill five black children, that is an act of individual racism, widely deplored by most segments of the society. But when in that same city – Birmingham, Alabama – five

> *hundred black babies die each year because of the
> lack of proper food, shelter and medical facilities,
> and thousands more are destroyed and maimed
> physically, emotionally and intellectually because
> of conditions of poverty and discrimination
> in the black community, that is a function of
> institutional racism. When a black family moves
> into a home in a white neighborhood and is
> stoned, burned or routed out, they are victims
> of an overt act of individual racism which many
> people will condemn - at least in words. But it is
> institutional racism that keeps black people locked
> in dilapidated slum tenements, subject to the daily
> prey of exploitative slumlords, merchants, loan
> sharks and discriminatory real estate agents. The
> society either pretends it does not know of this
> latter situation, or is in fact incapable of doing
> anything meaningful about it.*
>
> **—Stokely Carmichael, Black Power:The
> Politics of Liberation**

Civil rights activist, Stokely Carmichael, coined the term *institutional racism* in the 1960s when many white moderates wanted to focus on the transformation of attitudes among individual whites. Carmichael asserted that much more toxic than personal bias was institutional bias which constitutes a pattern of institutions such as banks, governmental organizations, courts, schools, and neighborhoods treating a particular group of people negatively based on race. Since the inception of the Civil Rights movement of the twentieth century, activists have emphasized the need for changing both our individual and institutional attitudes toward people of color. Millions of white Americans have experienced very dramatic transformations in their attitudes toward and relationships with minorities, but institutional patterns persist and in the second decade of the twenty-first century continue to influence the wellbeing of blacks, Hispanics, Asians, and other minorities in the United States.

In the throes of protests throughout the United States in December, 2014 following grand jury rulings on the shooting of unarmed black teenager Michael Brown in Ferguson, Missouri four months prior and the suffocation death of Eric Garner at the hands of New York City police in July, 2014, Eric Draitser stated in his Russia TV online article, "Racial Discrimination Is Deeply Embedded In Fabric of The US Society"[29]:

> *It's hard to say if you are making an argument that an institution is, by its very nature and form, an oppressive force, that's one thing. But just on the level of reform, the fact of the matter is here in New York City we had a "progressive" mayor elected, and as his first action he appointed one of the most reactionary and villainous figures in recent NYPD history, Will Bratton, to head the police force here, someone with quite a long reputation of racially discriminatory policies, such as the so-called "broken windows policing" here in New York City. So if you want to start to address the problem even just as a first step, you can begin to ask yourself what are we – that is to say the City of New York, City of Saint Louis or Los Angeles, whatever – what are we as a city doing to address what is undeniably a problem that is faced by a vast swath of the population of the city? We are talking about major American cities*

with major demographic issues, demographics that show massive portions of the city are African American, massive portions of the city that see the police as an occupying force, not as one that is there to protect them. So you have to address a sociological phenomenon before you can start any high- minded talk about reform.

In a 2015 interview by Luke Brinker for Salon Magazine, linguist and left-wing activist Noam Chomsky astutely analyzed America's institutionalized racism in its historical context.

Chomsky states:

"The first black slaves were brought to the colonies 400 years ago. We cannot allow ourselves to forget that during this long period there have been only a few decades when African-Americans, apart from a few, had some limited possibilities for entering the mainstream of American society.

"We also cannot allow ourselves to forget that the hideous slave labor camps of the new "empire of liberty" were a primary source for the wealth and privilege of American society, as well as England and the continent....The industrial revolution was based on cotton, produced primarily in the slave labor camps of the United States."

Throughout the country's history, Chomsky says, enforcers of racial subjugation have been gripped by fears that the oppressed will rebel against the racial hierarchy.

"Some of the slave-owners, like Jefferson, appreciated the moral turpitude on which the economy relied. But he feared the liberation of slaves, who have 'ten thousand recollections' of the crimes to which they were subjected. Fears that the victims might rise up and take revenge are deeply rooted in American culture, with reverberations to the present."

The harsh realities of American racism and how it functions are seldom acknowledged, Chomsky argues—the willful result of national myth-making and truth-shrouding.

"There is also a common variant of what has sometimes been called 'intentional ignorance' of what it is inconvenient to know: 'Yes, bad things happened in the past, but let us put all of that behind us and march on to a glorious future, all sharing equally in the rights and opportunities of citizenry.,"[30]

In the preceding paragraph, Chomsky is describing our compulsion to bury the collective shadow of racism in our past and focus only on the strides we have made since the end of the Civil War. However, Jung warned that, "Unfortunately there can be no doubt that man is, on the whole, less good than he imagines himself or wants to be. Everyone carries a shadow, and the less it is embodied in the individual's conscious life, the blacker and denser it is. If an inferiority is conscious, one always has a chance to correct it. Furthermore, it is constantly in contact with other interests, so that it is continually subjected to modifications. But if it is repressed and isolated from consciousness, it never gets corrected."[31]

The eruption of racial tension in the United States in the second decade of the twenty-first century appears to eerily echo Jung's incisive caveat.

During the protests across the United States in response to the Brown and Garner deaths, frequent slogans shouted and written on placards were "I can't breathe"—the last words of Eric Garner as he was being subdued by New York police officers, and "Black Lives Matter"—a response to the deaths of both men. The Black Lives Matter website states: "Black Lives Matter is an ideological and political intervention in a world where Black lives are systematically and intentionally targeted for demise. It is an affirmation of Black folks' contributions to this society, our humanity, and our resilience in the face of deadly oppression."[32]

How is it that 150 years after the conclusion of the American Civil War, we are witnessing an epidemic of young black men being shot by white police officers and an ensuing upheaval of protest in American society in response to these atrocities? In 1992 the City of Los Angeles erupted in massive riots following the acquittal of four Los Angeles Police Department officers who had stopped Rodney King for speeding, then subsequently tased and brutally beat him while he was lying on the ground. The beating was caught on camera and became an iconic example of American police brutality. Other than the Rodney King incident, rioting and protests with regard to race relations in the United States have been sparse since the turbulent years of the Civil Rights Movement—until now.

The recent rash of police brutality incidents in the

black community have occurred alongside the dramatic militarization of police in America. In recent years, since the conclusion of the Iraq War and the winding down of the War in Afghanistan, the Pentagon has issued unprecedented amounts of military equipment to local police departments, presumably because it does not want excess equipment sitting idly in mothballs while local police could be utilizing it. Concurrently, the training of local police officers has taken on more of the flavor of permanent combat, as if police officers are not just protecting the community but are actually engaged in war. In her August 30, 2014 article in Salon Magazine, "Militarized Police Are Everywhere," Ann Hagedorn states, "When police officers are armed and trained like soldiers, it's not surprising that they act like soldiers."[33]

The juxtaposition of increased police aggression against the African American community in the United States and the militarization of police throughout the nation depicts the reality of two enormous American shadows playing out in tandem. In terms of racism, Americans have never fully come to terms with the institution of slavery. Inasmuch as excellent historical accounts have been written and portrayed in film and other media, few white Americans have absorbed the horror of slavery and experienced the agonizing remorse necessary to commit to the journey of confronting personal and institutional racism. While white Americans revere Dr. Martin Luther King, Jr. and enthusiastically celebrate his birthday every January, we have been seduced, in my opinion, into the illusion that the Civil Rights Movement he spearheaded resolved the race issue, and that we can now put it behind us. At this writing, however, the nation is once again being torn apart by racial strife. The names of young black men murdered by white police officers, the cacophony of protest, and the horrific assassination of two New York City Police officers by an African American man in December 2014 in retaliation for the deaths of Michael Brown, Eric Garner, and others, are searing reminders that nothing has been put behind us.

Institutional racism is the elephant in the room that has never been sufficiently addressed by white America. While talking heads on cable news channels debate the use of body cameras by local police officers as the magic bullet (no pun intended) that will alleviate police brutality, and as white Americans attempt to convince themselves that yet again, technology is our savior, no one is seriously discussing institutional racism—the shadow of all make-nice appearances of racial harmony and healing since the glory days of the Civil Rights Movement.

In his December, 2014 Common Dreams article, "What Ferguson, Eric Garner, and CIA Torture Have in Common," Shahid Buttar, notes that "Parallels between CIA torture and police murders in New York, Ferguson, Cleveland, and elsewhere may be easy to overlook. Unfortunately, both sets of abuses reflect similar patterns: severe crimes committed by powerful people, officially endorsed cover-ups, and formal legal impunity that compounds the original crimes."

If directly questioned about their attitudes toward people of color or their misuse of power, the CIA contractor/torturer is likely to insist that he is not racist and that he was only doing his job. Likewise, the white Cleveland police officer who on November 22, 2014, shot and killed twelve-year-old Tamir Rice as Tamir was playfully brandishing an air gun, would deny fear of young black males and swear that he was merely attempting to protect and serve the community. Meanwhile, an epidemic of deaths of young black males at the hands of white police officers continues with the ghastly murder of Eric Harris in April 2015 by a poorly- trained white reserve police officer, and the death days later of Freddie Gray in Baltimore—a twenty-five year-old black man arrested by police and who sustained a severe neck injury during detention that severed his spinal cord, ultimately resulting in his death.

On the other end of the shadow's spectrum, we have voices such as Nicole Wallace, former White House Communication Chief during the George W. Bush Administration. With respect to America's torture program, Wallace shamelessly states, "I don't care what we did." And of course, former Vice President Dick Cheney says he'd torture again in a heartbeat.

While it is useful to view the historical events that have led up to the present moment and connect the dots, it is equally useful, and I believe, necessary, to view current manifestations of the shadow in terms of the collapse of empire. Exceptionalism, entitlement, and excesses of power tend to exacerbate as civilizations crumble. "I was just doing my job" and "I'm a cop; my job is to protect and serve" are simply shadow defenses that seek to justify brutal behavior with no intention whatever of altering it.

The United States leads the world in the number of people incarcerated. With financing from Wall Street, for-profit prison companies seek to keep their jails full and expand them. Likewise, we lead the world in police brutality. We are second-to-none in terms of police killing civilians.

Surely, we're not South Africa under apartheid, we say as we attempt to rationalize current events. Ethnic cleansing only happens in places like Bosnia, right? Meanwhile, the institutional racism we refuse to address within ourselves and within our communities, the terror of young black males and the terror of a society out of control that must be subdued with increasingly sophisticated military hardware—all of this is the American shadow writ large across a disintegrating empire.

Jungian analyst Sylvia Brinton Perera has written extensively on the Scapegoat archetype. "Scapegoating," according to Perera, "as it is currently practiced, means finding the one or ones who can be identified with evil or wrong-doing, blamed for it, and cast out from the community in order to leave the remaining members with a feeling of guiltlessness, atoned (at-one) with the collective standards of behavior."[34] Scapegoating is a form of denying the shadow. What is seen as unfit to conform to the ego ideal is split off and called "evil" or "undesirable," or, as Barry Spector names it, "the Other." Whether the one scapegoated rejects the attribution or not, Perera notes that they will inevitably feel its sting and "may unconsciously feel responsible for more than their personal share of shadow."[35]

So how do we cease scapegoating, and what are the rewards of doing so? Jung suggested that struggling with one's own shadow and becoming brutally honest regarding one's own scapegoating of the other (including opening to ways we do this of which we may not be fully aware) is the beginning of the healing journey. Jungian analyst Erich Neumann more specifically suggested:

> *In contrast to scapegoat psychology, in which the individual eliminates his own evil by projecting it on to the weaker brethren, we now find that the exact opposite is happening: we encounter the phenomenon of "vicarious suffering." The individual assumes personal responsibility for part of the burden on the collective, and he decontaminates this evil by integrating it into his own inner process of transformation. If the operation is successful, it leads to an inner liberation of the collective, which in part at least is redeemed from this evil.*[36]

Within this astringent shadow work lies the possibility of personal transformation, enabled by a willingness to deeply ponder the qualities within oneself that one is projecting outward. Equally important is deep grief regarding one's scapegoating behavior, and a willingness to form authentic relationships with those one has "Othered." As a result, not only personal healing, but healing of the larger community is possible.

In his article "An Archetypal Dilemma: The LA Riots," Jerome Bernstein notes that in Western culture, skin color plays a powerful role in the projection of our nation's shadow. "The darker the skin color, the greater the shadow projections and the worse the discrimination."[37] He suggests that, "In a psycho-spiritual sense, a culture that subscribes to a religious gospel that holds that its principle god is one who 'is light and in him is no darkness at all' very much loads the relative value of light and dark in that society."[38]

From Bernstein's perspective, "Blacks as a group carry the collective shadow of the culture as a whole. This archetypal fact, in my view, accounts for the extraordinary rage and hopelessness at the core of the collective unconscious of the Black community in this country… Nothing will heal the alienation with the Black community of this country that does not recognize and take responsibility for the fact that Blacks have been and remain the permanent scapegoat of our culture in ways that are manifested in no other minority group…As the archetypal scapegoat of the dominant culture they remain caught in a dilemma from which there is seemingly no escape, where virtually all the cards are in the hands of the perceived persecutor. As long as they are the scapegoats, the Black community will remain the outcast of the nation, forever used to carry the country's sins. Having been cut off from their roots, with literally no place to go, the disenfranchised are strongly predisposed to rebel against their assigned role with violent rage."[39]

Following the Civil Rights Movement of the 1960s, significant gains were made by African Americans: economically, socially, politically, and educationally. Yet the core shadow issue of white-black relations was never addressed. An African American President of the ruling elite who abhors conflict and seeks to maintain the image of a "rational" former Professor of Constitutional Law shows little interest in entering the raging waters of America's scapegoating of the Black community. Rather, he appears to assume that by virtue of his election to the Presidency and an election to a second term, race relations in the United States have made such enormous strides that the nation need not enter the messiness of untangling what four centuries of scapegoating have wrought.

The shadow is relentless in seducing us into easy answers

that are not answers at all. Surely, the election of an African American President will produce overnight a post-racial society. At the shadow's behest, we preen and pontificate and pride ourselves in our advancement. How far we have come since Dr. King's "I Have A Dream" speech! Yet that great Black Lion of the Civil War era, Frederick Douglass, would unapologetically confront our blithe dismissal of what is required to heal the racial divide:

> *If there is no struggle, there is no progress. Those who profess to favor freedom, and yet deprecate agitation, are men who want crops without plowing up the ground. They want rain without thunder and lightning. They want the ocean without the awful roar of its many waters. This struggle may be a moral one; or it may be a physical one; or it may be both moral and physical; but it must be a struggle. Power concedes nothing without a demand. It never did and it never will.*[40]

SUGGESTED PRACTICES/EXERCISES: I believe that every individual on Earth who is not a person of color carries some aspect of racism is his/her psyche. In addition, many people of color harbor attitudes of "Othering" toward other people of color as well as those who are not persons of color. These specific attitudes of "Othering" have been passed down through countless generations for centuries, and inflicted on human beings of different ethnicities whom we fear or scapegoat. Healing our tendencies to "Other" our fellow humans is, I believe, a lifelong process, but the rewards of engaging in the process are incalculable. A host of resources for understanding the dynamics of oppression and deepening our compassion, as well as our sense of one-ness with all human beings, are readily available.

1) I highly recommend viewing the 1994 documentary "The Color of Fear" by filmmaker Lee Mun Wah, produced by Stir Fry Seminars [www.stirfryseminars. com/] in the San Francisco Bay Area. This powerful dialog among a small, multicultural group of men is a deeply moving exploration of conscious and unconscious "Othering," and also includes breakthrough moments of healing and union. The entire documentary may be viewed online. ["The Color of Fear" www.vimeo.com/102286311]

2) I suggest extensive journaling after watching this documentary, paying particular attention to the feelings it evokes and especially moments when you feel defensive, angry, impatient, or sad. Also notice the moments that warmed your heart. After viewing the documentary the first time, a more challenging exercise might be viewing it with a multicultural group of friends and reflecting together on your experiences.

3) Contemplate Chapter 3, "Interbeing," from Charles Eisenstein's book The More Beautiful World Our Hearts Know Is Possible (which may be read in book form or at www.charleseisenstein.net/books/the-more-beautiful-world-our-hearts-know-is-possible/

interbeing/). Eisenstein describes the focus of the chapter as follows: "The fundamental precept of the new story is that we are in-separate from the universe, and our being partakes in the being of everyone and everything else." To what extent have you experienced inter-being in relation to other humans and the Earth community? How has that influenced your life? What challenges have you encountered in practicing inter-being?

4) Highly recommended are books and trainings by Tim Wise, author of Dear White America: A Letter to a New Minority. Additionally recommended are specific racial justice trainings such as those offered by the Social Justice Institute, the Aspen Institute, various local branches of the YWCA, and the Racial Justice Training Institute of the Shriver National Center on Poverty Law.

Chapter 5

Thank You for your Service

THE ENDURING GHOSTS OF WAR

PTSD is presently classified as a "stress and anxiety disorder." But "stress and anxiety" does not begin to describe the emotions people experience during warfare. We don't really have words for it. Also PTSD classifies veterans as "disabled" by how far they are from the civilian norm. But veterans are not disabled civilians. They are war-wounded soldiers and have different values and expectations about life. When we require that they get on with "business as usual" now that they are home, we put the blame on them for having broken down in the first place, and we pressure them to take sole responsibility for their healing. But everyone who participates in a war is changed. No one comes through unscathed.

—Ed Tick,"Like Wandering Ghosts"

Historically, veterans of US wars are not well-honored. As far back as the Revolutionary War, a denial of their pain and a lack of emotional and economic support are shamefully obvious. We pay elaborate lip service to the "war hero" in this culture, but once he or she has accomplished the mission, they are easily discarded and become as ordinary as any citizen who has never spent one hour on the battlefield.

In the Iraq War from 2003-2010, more than 155,000 Iraqi civilians were killed as well as more than 3,000 US troops. In addition, more than 32, 000 US troops were wounded, and currently, nearly 22 veterans of US wars commit suicide every day.[41] Behind the *glory* stories of military recruitment publicity and "support the troops" hysteria are *gory* stories of hundreds of thousands of shattered bodies and psyches. These are the shadows of military heroism and guilt-laden propaganda campaigns that attempt to convince us that "freedom isn't free."

The vibrant eighteen year-old who craves an authentic initiation by the elders of his community where none is to be found, his body reverberating with the hot blood of heroism; or perhaps the young man who knows that through his military service, he will become an American citizen—despite everything either young man may know about the devastations of soldiers returning from war, each enthusiastically walks out of the recruiter's office and into a permanently life-altering underworld journey. Throughout his basic training, a young man discovers the thrill of enervating physical conditioning and the intoxication of entrance into a brotherhood of warrior comrades. Undeterred by bland food and meager pay, he is delirious with the role of "professional soldier."

At this moment in his young life, no amount of logic or statistics could convince him that he is a pawn—putty in the hands of a military-industrial-security state that will profit lavishly from the war in which he will fight and by which he will be permanently devastated. Should he encounter a war protestor, he would risk life and limb to correct their "anti-patriotic" views. Isn't this what manhood is all about? Fighting for the values of America, being part of a brotherhood of warriors, making one's family proud, being willing to pay the supreme sacrifice for one's country?

Tragically, this young man, should he survive physically, is likely to return home in two or three years with body parts missing and a psyche shredded by the horrors of war. He will continue to applaud his branch of service and particularly his combat unit. He will be a man whose insides have been hollowed out by trauma and loss. Perhaps no day will pass that he does not contemplate suicide. He will likely to be taking a host of medications; he will not sleep well at night; and he will find previous relationships with family and civilian friends exceedingly difficult to maintain. His body is "home," but his soul is not. He may obsess about his combat unit and how he should have done more for them —how he should have saved more lives, or how he didn't deserve to survive in the midst of the carnage.

Psychotherapist Ed Tick, who specializes in working with war veterans, states, "Moral and spiritual trauma is at the core of PTSD, and no matter how well-intentioned various therapies are—such as cognitive-behavioral therapy, stress-reduction techniques, and medications— none takes on the moral and spiritual dimensions. Therapies like these can sometimes be helpful in restoring everyday functioning, but they do not bring healing. We need public apologies, public confessions, and public grief for all that we have done to our veterans, to other nations, and to the earth."

In his book *The Hidden Spirituality Of Men: Ten Metaphors To Awaken The Sacred Masculine*, Matthew Fox states: that this culture has never understood the difference between the warrior and the soldier archetypes.

> *To me, the key is understanding the distinction between a warrior and a soldier. A Vietnam veteran who volunteered to go to war at 17 described this eloquently: "When I was in the army, I was a soldier. I was a puppet doing whatever anybody told me to do, even if it meant going against what my heart told me was right. I didn't know nothing about being a warrior until I hit the streets and marched alongside my brothers for something I really believed in. When I found something I believed in, a higher power found me." He quit being a soldier and became a warrior when he followed his soul's orders, not his officer's; in his case, this meant protesting war and going to jail for it. The late Buddhist meditation master Chögyam Trungpa talks about the "sad and tender heart of the warrior." The warrior is in touch with his heart—the joy, the sadness, the expansiveness of it.*[42]

Ed Tick describes the approach he takes in working with veterans, and the perspective of some indigenous peoples in relating to men returning from war:

> *I use treatments given to warriors in traditional cultures, which expected that the invisible wounds of war would be deep, penetrating, and transformative. Indigenous cultures limited the extent of warfare and its damage, and they*

watched over their warriors in the midst of battle and after their return. For example, among the Papago [Tohono O'odham] people of the American Southwest, after a warrior had his first experience of combat, they held a nineteen-day ceremony of return. He might have been in battle for fifteen minutes, and for that he'd get almost three weeks of ritual healing and community support. He'd be put in isolation and not allowed to touch food or feed himself, because he'd been poisoned by the war experience. He couldn't see his family, and he certainly couldn't have sex with his wife, or else he would bring the war pollution back into the community. Elders and medicine people used purification techniques to cleanse him, and also storytelling techniques, which we would call "expressive-arts therapy." The war dance wasn't what Hollywood portrays it as: a bunch of savages whipping themselves into a frenzy before battle. It came after battle and was a dramatic reenactment of the conflict for the tribe.

Instead of having a parade and going shopping, we could use our veterans' holidays as an occasion for storytelling. Open the churches and temples and synagogues and mosques and community centers and libraries across the country, and invite the veterans in to tell their stories. Purification ceremonies and storytelling events are also opportunities for the community to speak to veterans and take some of the burden of guilt off them and declare our oneness with them: "You killed in our name, because we ordered you to, so we take responsibility for it, too."

The final step is initiation into the warrior class. We need to train our veterans in the warrior tradition and not just expect them to behave as typical civilians. Many of them can't, but they are looking for ways to be of service. Labeling a veteran "100 percent disabled" only ensures that he or she is not going to do anything for the rest of his or her life.

Traditional societies understood that warriorhood is not soldiering but a path through life — a "warrior's path," not a "warpath." In traditional societies, warriors strove to live up to the highest moral standards. They hated the destruction caused by war, and they sought to preserve what was precious to them. They served as police during times of peace and used violence only as a last resort. They had responsibilities that kept them busy throughout their lives, including mentoring younger men.[43]

Going to war, being wounded, and returning from battle is a profound emotional and spiritual initiation. Unfortunately, it is a profane initiation not intended or structured to transform consciousness and mindfully transition the soldier from childhood to adulthood. In fact, the initiation is carried out by the wrong people at the wrong time, for all the wrong reasons. It mindlessly catapults the young person into battle where "good" and "evil" are superficially assigned to the warring sides, and the principal concern is the triumph of "us" over "them." In combat training, the state attempts to dictate morality and convince the soldier that the taking of innocent lives is simply the collateral damage that goes with the territory and that somehow they will be forgiven for committing atrocities. However, Tick notes:

> *Almost all of us want to be agents of good. For many soldiers the motive for being a warrior is not to kill and destroy, but to preserve and protect. Then they find themselves in immoral wars where they are forced to be agents of destruction. I was recently discussing this issue with army chaplains, and I asked what they did to counsel soldiers who have just come back from a firefight or have committed atrocities. One chaplain said, "I teach my soldiers that they have to renegotiate their covenant with God." The assumption that God's going to forgive us for, say, killing a child just because we had no choice doesn't wash with many soldiers. Their relationship with the divine is quite often damaged. As the chaplain said, they have to renegotiate it. Veterans and soldiers have to find ways to reconnect with the divine and undo that moral inversion and become again agents of creation.[44]*

Thus the soldier returning from combat is psychically shattered not only by the trauma of war, but by the incessant moral dilemmas that war foists upon everyone in its wake.

Nor does the moral burden weigh only on male soldiers. Tick notes how female soldiers suffer emotionally and spiritually the wounds of war:

> *Many women are suffering terribly in the combat zone. One woman veteran I've met returned*

home from Iraq in a horrible depression because she had machine-gunned women and children. She refused help and was redeployed. She told her family she wanted the Iraqis to kill her as punishment for what she had done to them.

Some women veterans suffer because they feel they were created to be life givers, not life takers. So the moral trauma of war is more severe for them. But if we understand the warrior's role to be not destroying and killing, but preserving and protecting, then we can find many women serving honorably in our military. Some of the most admirable women I have ever met are combat nurses, chaplains, and career officers.

There have been traditional cultures with women warriors and chiefs. Some Northwest Native American tribes had women warriors who were combatants. Among the Iroquois, clan mothers were given the ultimate power to declare war, because they were the ones who'd given birth to those who would be sent into battle.[45]

Yet a female soldier need not enter combat to exit the military with massive Post-Traumatic Stress Disorder (PTSD). The sexual assault of women in the military has skyrocketed in recent years. A Mother Jones Magazine photo series on "Women Who Risked Everything to Expose Sexual Assault in the Military" reports, "Women in the US military are being raped and sexually assaulted by their colleagues in record numbers. An estimated 26,000 rapes and sexual assaults took place in the military in 2012, the last year that statistics are available; only one in seven victims reported their attacks, and just one in ten of those cases went to trial. According to mental health experts, the effects of Military Sexual Trauma (MST) include depression, substance abuse, paranoia, and feelings of isolation. Victims spend years drowning in shame and fear as the psychological damage silently eats away at their lives. Many frequently end up addicted to drugs and alcohol, homeless, or take their own lives."[46]

> Not only are women in the military incessantly vulnerable to sexual assault, but when it occurs, it is frequently not reported—because prosecutions of offenders are rare, the chain of command appears to allow it, and female victims often believe that reporting is futile.

> Michael Meade, founder of the Mosaic Multicultural Foundation, which offers retreats uniting returning veterans and their families, also elaborates on the ghosts of war:

> *Even those who found a sense of purpose in going to war can wind up lost upon return and living on life's anguished margin. Leave all the politics aside, whether a war is deemed successful or disastrous, the effects of battle continue to rage inside the soldiers in wounds that torture the body, in dreams that shatter common reality, and in traumas that continue to trouble the soul. Veterans can become literally homeless— abandoned in and by their own communities after*

sacrificing parts of their bodies and souls for their homeland.

There is a great and growing disconnection that leaves many men and women out in the cold, unable to adapt to civilian circumstances, feeling unwelcome in the exact communities they intended to serve. Make no mistake, the war always comes home with the warriors and too often makes simply being at home impossible. As one officer wrote at a recent retreat for vets, "I walked down my ramp alone, returning to a reception of none. No welcome home party, because like so many others, I'm not home."[47]

THE CULTURE OF WAR

Chris Hedges in *War Is A Force That Gives Us Meaning*, states that "The rush of battle is a potent and often lethal addiction, for war is a drug."[48] Hedges elaborates on the culture of war, asserting that it offers "excitement, exoticism, power, chances to rise above our small stations in life, and a bizarre and fantastic universe that has a grotesque and dark beauty."

The reality of brutality in combat and the manner in which some individuals become addicted to it is inherent in war, and has been characteristic of all wars throughout history. But most compelling to me in considering the personal and collective shadows is how modern war is manufactured, packaged, delivered, and sold to the masses as necessary, as the lesser of two evils and something on which we are assured our lives depend.

In his extraordinary book *The Evil Hours: A Biography*

Of Post-Traumatic Stress Disorder, ex-Marine and Iraq War veteran David Morris offers a stunningly brilliant assessment of the collective shadow of the war on terror and the attendant PTSD that resides in the psyches of Americans since September 11, 2001:

> *It would be foolish to diagnose an entire nation with a mental health disorder, but as Susan Faludi points out in her 2007 book The Terror Dream: Fear and Fantasy in Post 9/11 America, the country as a whole continues to exhibit certain aspects of post-traumatic stress, including a compulsion to re-enact the events of September 11 in movies and television, as well as nurturing obsessions with homeland security and surveillance that, according to many military analysts, is out of proportion with the actual threat and smacks of a kind of national hypervigilance. Moreover, the ongoing militarization of American culture—in the form of first-person shooter video games, the rise of the Navy SEAL "brand" in books, films, and other media, and martially themed endurance races like the Tough Mudder series—points to a fixation with the post 9/11 hyper-masculinity and ubiquitous violence reminiscent of the disorder.*[49]

As noted above, war provides a profane initiation for young men who are hungering for one that is actually sacred and soul-enhancing. Additionally, war seduces humans to believe that by engaging in it, they are opting for higher moral ground. Deluded by the polarity of good vs. evil, the human ego becomes inflated with the "righteousness" of its cause and the "wickedness" of the enemy. The Savior archetype (as noted in Chapter 2 in the discussion of power dynamics of Victim/Tyrant/Rebel/ Savior) becomes constellated, attended by the cultural injunction to "protect and serve." Suddenly, ethical justifications for doing whatever it takes to win are legion, and the collective unconsciously colludes in the notion that the end justifies the means. The definition of the word collusion is instructive because it literally means the sharing of an illusion. The shadow's projection mission is accomplished when the masses have become convinced that their military and political objective is not only honorable but irreproachable, and that at the end of the day, they are essentially "doing God's work." To this end, myriad propaganda techniques demonizing the enemy are invaluable tools for perpetuating the collusion.

As industrial civilization continues to wither, along with a planet raped, pillaged, and plundered for its resources, we can anticipate ongoing wars, endless wars, and wars that destroy not only human lives, but ravage the economies and infrastructures of both defeated nations and triumphant ones. Yet the culture of war could not endure without the personal and collective shadows that rationalize the carnage and periodically resuscitate the chimera of an impeccably professional military that exceeds all other nations in caring for its wounded.

However, the assertion that the United States government cares for its wounded warriors well is unequivocally false. In a trenchant 2015 article entitled "Troop Worship," journalist Abby Martin notes:

> *As of March 2014 the backlog of veterans' benefits was a staggering 400,000 cases with an average wait time of 125 days to process the claims,*

according to the Iraq and Afghanistan Veterans of America. At least one million servicemen and women have been injured in Iraq and Afghanistan, compared to 300 thousand during the Vietnam War, despite the lack of a draft. The number could be even higher, but the VA abruptly stopped publishing the number of injured troops, citing national security reasons for the censorship.

The disgraceful way veterans are treated in this country exemplifies how little this government actually values life. Amidst all the ritualistic pageantry immortalizing fallen soldiers, we lose sight of the military mind, one that dominates policy and breeds new generations of sadists, who are taught that other human beings have lesser value than them. This toxic mindset seeps into every facet of American society, teaching every citizen that force is the answer to every problem.[50]

Perhaps the worst trauma of war, the most intrusive and insistent ghost, is an inner knowing in the depths of the psyche that one has been deceived and betrayed by the designs of politicians and a national security-weapons industry that values only economic gain, resource acquisition, and geo-political hegemony. The betrayal experienced may appear in the guise of protest regarding the loss of benefits, or scandals in government bureaucracies that delay or undermine adequate medical care for veterans. However, these are only symptomatic of an empire that pays lip service to the wellbeing of its military personnel while seducing them into the culture of war. Conversely, when the shadow of "thank you for your service" is fully exposed, the wounded warrior has an opportunity to return to wholeness.

The *dark gold* in healing the ghosts of war is sometimes attained through an inner conflagration—a formidable journey into the warrior's heart that allows him or her to finally return home and experience a profound sense of belonging to family and community.

"Many traditional cultures," says Michael Meade, "developed ways to 'take the war out of the warriors.' Native American, African, Irish, and many other groups understood that those who send souls into battle must also retrieve those souls from the underworld of war. A genuine rite of return involves a caring and careful clearing of the soul as well as a thorough healing of the body. In years of working with vets I have found that no matter how confusing or devastating it may seem, the unique story of each veteran becomes the language for healing, the essential ground for recovery, and the path towards finding a renewed sense of purpose and meaning. Not only that, but the stories must be heard and the souls must be welcomed back by caring and compassionate representatives of the community that sent them off to war."[51]

David Morris argues that Post-Traumatic Stress Disorder is an affliction not exclusively of the individual veteran but of the society at large. In *The Evil Hours*, he informs the reader extensively of the variety of approaches to treatment of PTSD, and notes that the standard protocol in current time is a focus on the biology of the disorder with emphasis on "finding a cure." In response, Morris argues that "…if a 'cure' for post-traumatic stress can be found, then society as a whole won't have to bother with trying to deal with the events that cause trauma, which have deep roots in social justice issues."[52]

The enduring ghosts of war aren't only the nightmares, flashbacks, hypervigilance, insomnia, hair- trigger violence, emotional distance and psychic numbing of the tormented war veteran. These ghosts only echo and pantomime the ghosts of a society which remains detached from war other than to manufacture and applaud it. "These two worlds, war and home," says Morris, "could be kept isolated, one living in almost perfect ignorance of the other," which he says is "an obscenity surpassed only by the obscenity of the war itself."[53]

"Thank you for your service" rings hollow in the ears of the men and women who were valuable to society when enlisting, training, fighting, and dying, but have become hollowed-out, throw-away phantoms upon their return from war. The industrialization of war facilitates the distancing of citizens from those purportedly defending them. Or, in the incisive words of David Morris:

> *The industrialization of war is a relatively new phenomenon, and no other country sends as many men and women overseas to kill as we do. No other people in history has sent as many as far away with as little sacrifice demanded of the average citizen as we do. No other people in history is as disconnected from the brutality of war as the United States today. Were the truth of war to become apparent to Americans, we wouldn't continue to train, equip, and deploy warriors the way we do. Nor would we ask them when they came home if they killed anyone.*[54]

THE WAR HERO VS. THE WAR VILLAIN

In July 2013, Private First Class Chelsea Manning, born Bradley Manning, a US Army Intelligence Specialist, was convicted of violations of the Espionage Act and sentenced to 35 years in prison. Manning released thousands of secret documents to WikiLeaks, an international, non-profit journalistic organization founded by Julian Assange, which specializes in exposing government secrets. Among the secrets exposed by Manning were an official policy by the US government to ignore torture in Iraq; the systematic cover up of child abuse by military contractors in Afghanistan; the overwhelming innocence of the majority of men detained at the Guantanamo Bay Detention Camp; US military officials withholding information about the indiscriminate killing of Reuters journalists and innocent Iraqi civilians; known Egyptian torturers who received training from the FBI in Quantico, Virginia; the fact that the Japanese and US Governments had been warned about the seismic threat at Fukushima; and the Obama Administration allowing Yemen's President to cover up a secret US drone bombing campaign.

The whistleblower, whether it be Chelsea Manning, Edward Snowden, Coleen Rowley, Daniel Ellsberg, or a host of other men and women throughout history, is the one who exposes the shadow of some entity that is deceiving, oppressing, or betraying the masses. The archetype of the whistleblower is ancient and deeply imbedded in our consciousness. Socrates was the philosophical gadfly of Athens who demanded that citizens contemplate meaning and purpose. In the Greek myth of Cassandra, it was said that Apollo gave her the power of prophecy in order to seduce her, but when she refused him, he gave her the curse of never being believed. Like Cassandra, the whistleblower, or simply the inconspicuous activist, may have the courage and discernment to expose the shadow, but there will always be a price to pay. He or she will always be vilified in some manner.

As anonymously stated in James Fallows' January 2015 *Atlantic* article, "The Tragedy of The American Military," a man who worked for decades overseeing Pentagon contracts stated, "The system is based on lies and self- interest, purely toward the end of keeping money moving." According to this former Pentagon official, what kept the system running was that "the services get their budgets, the contractors get their deals, the Congressmen get jobs in their districts, and no one who's not part of the deal bothers to find out what is going on."[55]

This succinct description of the US military summarizes how it functions and to what end. When the shadow is not exposed, it produces many ghosts, such as the ghosts of war. When it is exposed, its collateral damage in terms of lives permanently altered or destroyed is vast and often incalculable. Just as the military insists that "freedom isn't free," exposure of the shadow often takes a brutal toll. Losing one's job as a result of whistleblowing is often the least of one's woes. Many truth-tellers have lost incredible amounts of money; been victimized by extortion or arson; endured bankruptcy and the loss of all material possessions; received death threats; succumbed to chronic, catastrophic illnesses; and many have been murdered or found dead as a result of an "apparent" suicide. Choosing to expose the truth about a government, an institution, or a corporate behemoth may literally cost the whistleblower everything—including their life, and almost always catapults the truth-teller into an underworld initiation of suffering, alienation, and excruciating dilemmas of meaning and purpose.

Yet many report that speaking the truth was the most pivotal and defining moment of their lives. In spite of all it cost them, they could not have done otherwise. Not infrequently, the shadow's tentacles can reach so far into our lives that we cannot extricate ourselves from them without losing parts of ourselves. Yet the dark gold is discovered when we realize that our truth-telling has made us someone we no longer recognize, but whom we joyously embrace, because we did what we came here to accomplish.

— — — — — — — — — — —

SUGGESTED PRACTICES: Endless war or endless military campaigns are spawned by adolescent psyches that have not experienced sacred initiation. In this culture, we do not provide our youth with formal initiation rites, but rather, individuals are left on their own, devoid of community support, with painful initiatory moments that shape their lives for better or worse. Rarely do people make conscious sense of such moments.

1) Take time to reflect, perhaps by journaling, about initiatory moments in your youth—times of grief, loss, tragedy, violence, or other forms of wounding that altered your life or even shattered your soul. Were there any mentors in your life? Throughout these experiences, what did you learn about yourself?

What decisions did you make about what it means to be a man or a woman in this culture?

2) Every human being carries both a feminine shadow and a masculine shadow. A 2013 article by Gary Stamper entitled "Creating The New Story: The Masculine and The Feminine," may be useful in explaining this concept. After reading the article, you may want to consider these questions: What do you know about your masculine and feminine shadows? If you are a man, what do you know about your sacred masculine self? If you are a woman, what do you know about your sacred feminine self?[56]

3) Carl Jung asserted that the outer world reflects the inner landscape. Terrorism moved to center stage in terms of geopolitical events after September 11, 2001. For the past 15 years, the United States and the world have become preoccupied with terrorism. Each individual who aspires to be spiritually awake must address the following two questions: *Who is my "inner terrorist?* and *How does this terrorist disturb my internal 'homeland security'*? Consider reflecting and journaling extensively on these questions.

4) How do you project your fear, anger, sorrow, anxiety, disappointment or other difficult emotions onto other people or groups of people? How do you see industrially civilized cultures projecting their dark emotions on indigenous or tribal cultures and people of color?

5) Return to the exercise at the end of Chapter 2 in which you were asked to track your own personal Victim/Tyrant/ Rebel/Savior dynamic. (also see Appendix) Taking this dynamic to the next big-picture level, how do you see the nations involved in current geopolitical conflicts acting out this dynamic?

6) Every power structure has a shadow, including systems like schools, churches, companies, and organizations— even humanitarian organizations. This is not wrong, but merely inevitable. Choose a particular power structure with which you are familiar. Describe its shadow. How is the system's shadow oppressive to people or to the Earth? What secrets are being harbored? What pieces of truth are not being told?

CHAPTER 6

THE SHADOW OF THE AMERICAN DREAM: THE ASSAULT ON HOME

The moral angle to the foreclosure crisis—and, of course, in capitalism we're not supposed to be concerned with the moral stuff, but let's mention it anyway—shows a culture that is slowly giving in to a futuristic nightmare ideology of computerized greed and unchecked financial violence.

—Matt Taibbi, The Divide: Injustice In The Age of TheWealth Gap

Human beings inhabiting industrial civilization are not nomadic. We are socialized primarily in homes, and the concept of home is deeply imbedded in our psyches. Home is a way of organizing space in our minds; in turn, our psychological habitat is shaped by the spaces we live in. In fact, we say that home is where the heart is, and even when conflict is occurring at home, it is nevertheless a kind of fixed point in a changing universe. A home provides shelter and a place to which we can retreat from the external world—a place that we can make our own. For Carl Jung, symbols of houses or home appearing in dreams represented the dreamer's psyche. In that sense, in the realm of the unconscious mind, home is an external representation of who we are—so that when we lose our home, we lose a part of ourselves.

In the fall of 2008, a financial collapse reverberated through America and sent shock waves around the world. The world's economic landscape has never been the same since that moment. One of the best summaries of the diabolical aspect of the crash is articulated by Ralph Nader:

> *Wall Street's big banks and their financial networks that collapsed the US economy in 2008-2009 were saved with huge bailouts by the taxpayers, but these Wall Street Gamblers are still paid huge money and are again creeping toward reckless misbehavior. Their corporate crime wave strip-mined the economy for young workers, threw them on the unemployment rolls and helped make possible a low-wage economy that is draining away their ability to afford basic housing, goods, and services.*[57]

The 2008 economic crash was one of the largest transfers of wealth in the history of our species. Nader's assessment of what the meltdown accomplished for these twenty-first century robber barons summarizes the repercussions experienced by the 99% of Americans who did not engineer the disaster. Among the carnage that resulted from the collapse of the economy was the permanent evisceration of the middle class, a defining characteristic of which was the capacity to own a home. At this writing in 2015, the number of people in the United States who can afford to own a home has been dramatically reduced; particularly, among the millennial generation, and among older Americans who have become permanently unemployed or who lost significant retirement savings in the crash.

The American Dream evolved steadily throughout the nation's history, but reached its apotheosis in post-World War II America in the 1950s. While the Dream was never defined unanimously by the middle class, it essentially meant not only home ownership but also the ability to earn a living wage, the security of substantial health benefits assumed by one's employer, the opportunity to accumulate solid retirement savings, and the ability to pay for the college education of one's children. Naturally, the Dream was always more available to white Americans than minorities, and it never guaranteed entrance into the territory of the wealthiest 1% of the population, but it established a buffer between extreme poverty and extreme opulence. In the second decade of the twenty- first century, that buffer is rapidly vanishing.

As Nader notes, a low-wage economy rules the day, and middle class accoutrements such as employer-paid benefits, retirement savings, and an affordable college education are rapidly fading into the rear-view mirror of American history. Young Americans who graduate from college are instantly saddled with student loan debt in a job market where positions that even require a college degree are becoming increasingly scarce. Millions of millennials, now living in the basements of their parents' home, have lost all hope of ever owning a home of their own. Countless older Americans who have lost retirement savings or have become permanently under-employed or unemployed have sold their homes, often at a loss, because they can no longer afford home ownership.

With the financial collapse of 2008, the shadow of the American Dream is unveiled. Prior to this event, home ownership in the United States was virtually sacrosanct. Without attempting to explain in full here the sub-prime mortgage debacle that played a pivotal role in the collapse, suffice it to say the financial crisis resulted in the loss of homes for millions of Americans. As the economy was strip-mined, as Nader puts it, these individuals lost the equity in their homes and very often lost it alongside their jobs. Some were able to recover financially after a period of months or years and purchase another home. Others were permanently financially disabled and became long-term renters. Still others became homeless.

To lose one's home—literally, one's shelter and symbolically, one's sense of self and a sacred space that reflects one's inner world—is to lose part of one's identity on both the inner and outer planes. If one cannot find another home, then one wanders in a permanent state of tenuous shelter and partial identity. Not only did the housing crisis of 2008 result in millions of individuals losing their homes, but collectively, the nation began losing an integral aspect of the American Dream.

The shadow of the American Dream has always been homelessness. The roots of the dream grew out of the Great Depression when homelessness was rampant, and tens of thousands of individuals and families relocated within the United States in order to find work. Perhaps the most formidable fear of people who still had homes in that era was that they might become one of the countless hobos hopping freight trains, or be part of a family like the Joads in John Steinbeck's *Grapes of Wrath*, seemingly forever dispossessed of home.

When the American Dream burgeoned in the 1950s, a number of social service safety nets were in place. In the 1960s, food stamps became available, as well as a number of other social welfare programs. At that time it appeared that middle class Americans were developing a more robust sense of caring for each other and were becoming more willing to spend tax dollars to that end. Yet this incipient consciousness of the commons was irrevocably altered by the election of Ronald Reagan in 1980. A conservative Republican, Reagan was adamant that "government is the problem" and that funding for social services must be dramatically reduced. Individual responsibility, not the commons, was the core of his ideology. Although the de-institutionalizing of the mentally ill began in California in the 1950s, by the time Reagan became governor of the state in 1967, that policy was well in place and was solidified with Reagan's signing of the Lanterman-Petris-Short Act, which essentially ended all civil commitments to mental institutions in the state. According to MentalIllnessWatch.org, President Reagan drastically curtailed funding for mental health programs in the United States and set in motion an avalanche of homelessness among the mentally ill, for whom inpatient and outpatient services were no longer available.[58] A later chapter of this book offers a more detailed exploration of homelessness, but my emphasis at this juncture is on the symbolism of home in the individual and collective psyche and what happens to us when we are no longer "at home."

The shadow of the American Dream has always been

abject poverty, while the preeminent conduit to realizing the dream has been home ownership. The assault on "home" began for many mentally ill Americans in the 1980s with Reaganomics, while others found themselves excluded from the dream in the twenty-first century with a financial crisis engineered by thugs in suits who have succeeded in precluding home ownership for millions of Americans.

In recent years as more individuals have awakened to the collapse of industrial civilization and the reality that we cannot sustain infinite growth on a finite planet, many have opted to alter their living arrangements by downsizing and living simpler, more fulfilling lives. They have discovered that on a planet with a carrying capacity of perhaps two billion human beings, attempting to live the American Dream amid a world population approaching eight billion is sheer madness. For these individuals, the American Dream has been revealed for the nightmare that it is. For them, home is no longer so much about plots of land or building materials, but creating a living arrangement that provides safety, warmth, wellbeing, mutual caring, and respect for the Earth community. Once we awaken from the American Dream or any other chimera that similarly deludes us, we must open our ears and hearts to the cry of the Earth, for in fact, the Earth is our original home, and arguably, our dire planetary predicament has resulted from our estrangement from the Earth community. In doing so, we ask the Earth what it wants from us, and in responding, we are carried home—a home that cannot be assaulted and from which we cannot be evicted.

SUGGESTED PRACTICES: For many years I have noticed that the more quality time I spend in nature, particularly contemplative time, the less I feel attached to and dependent on *things*. Yet I do not wish to offer one more sermon on simplicity or downsizing. Rather, I offer the opportunity to experience what it feels like to live on the edge of creature comforts and to deepen our relationship with Earth as home.

1) Consider a vision quest experience in which you join with others in a group to spend several days in the wilderness. However, it will not be a genuine vision quest unless you spend some of that time, preferably at least one day and night, absolutely alone in silence. A number of options for vision quest experiences can be found online, but it is important to be familiar with the facilitator(s) and trust their expertise and experience.

2) Consider enrolling in Tom Brown's Tracker School [https://www.trackerschool.com/] which offers the opportunity to "dive more deeply into the skills necessary to make any wilderness environment your home."[59] These courses provide not only training in survival skills but allow students to deeply immerse themselves in the reality of Earth as home.

3) Volunteer to work with homeless people in some capacity in your local community. In addition to providing food, healthcare, or other services, allow yourself to engage in conversations with these folks. As you become better acquainted with them, acknowledge their survival skills and listen deeply

as they share their experiences. Be very present with them and remember that what you are listening for is not specific skills, but rather, an attitude of survival and the capacity to navigate outdoor living.

CHAPTER 7

EXTINCTION

BEYOND THE SHADOW OF DEATH

The point is simply this: you are welcome to analyse the scientific evidence for yourself and make your own assessment of the timeframe and the degree of severity of the threat. Perhaps human extinction will not occur until next century. But whether we define 'near term' as 2030, 2040 or even next century, human extinction is now a distinct possibility. And after 200,000 years of our species, calling this 'near term' seems reasonable.
—Robert Burrowes, "Why Is Near-Term Human Extinction Inevitable?"

Perhaps the noblest private act is the unheralded effort to return: to open our hearts once they've closed, to open our souls once they've shied away, to soften our minds once they've been hardened by the storms of our day.
—Mark Nepo Endless Practice: BecomingWhoYouWere Born To Be, 2015

Holocene, Anthropocene, catastrophic climate change,

self- reinforcing feedback loops, near-term human extinction. Once quirky concepts of non-conventional theoreticians or social critics, these words have permeated the lexicon of scientific discourse and mainstream media to such an extent that it is now virtually impossible to avoid them. Elizabeth Kolbert's 2014 *New York Times* best-seller *The Sixth Extinction: An Unnatural History* precludes the possibility that the "E" word can be avoided in any comprehensive conversation about climate change and the future of ecosystems. While a variety of Near-Term Extinction support groups have appeared and burgeoned on social media, few people devote much time or energy to the topic of extinction.

Yet this does not preclude its nagging influence in the psyche. Indeed, the notion of extinction and all of the emotions attended by it constitute an enormous shadow in the collective psyche—and perhaps the final one. Therefore, any substantial consideration of the shadow must include the shadow of extinction, which could be the shadow to end all shadows. Thus, I choose not to debate the concept of extinction itself—whether it will happen or when it might happen. For me, these curiosities are far less important than the shadow extinction casts on all living beings on this planet. For this reason, I chose for the theme song of my weekly radio show Leonard Cohen's "Everybody Knows," because, in fact, on some level, everyone does know the extent to which extinction is breathing down our collective necks.

For this reason, we must commit to working with the five categories of the collective and personal shadows as outlined by Andrew Harvey, explained in Chapter One of this book. The fact that humans are destroying the planet —and that they know this—floods us with dread and makes the collective and personal shadows even darker and more deadly. The potential of near-term human extinction created by our species lingers like a dark cloud of radioactive fallout in the collective shadow and as such has a demonic life of its own, exacerbating the treachery of the personal shadow of each individual.

Extinction supersedes all other issues confronting life on Earth, because it threatens to terminate that life permanently. Few humans can comprehend this reality, and therefore, few humans can engage the concept other than theoretically or superficially. To allow ourselves to absorb extinction and its ramifications is to be catapulted into a whirlpool of emotions, most notably anger, abject fear, and deep, deep grief. Taking extinction seriously compels us to confront our own mortality and the mortality of everyone and everything we hold dear. Like the death row inmate, we know that our end is imminent even if we do not know the exact date. We hold the hope that a miracle will occur and that we might receive a stay of execution, but barring that unlikely event, our days are numbered.

So why not just end it now? What is the point of persevering?

If we are going to confront the shadow of an extinction which may or may not happen this century, the first step is to stop arguing about when it might happen and return to the bedrock of our human condition which is that someday, whatever the cause, we are going to die. All other babble about the correctness of the theory of near-term extinction or what year it might succeed in eliminating life on Earth is a frantic attempt to circumvent the inevitability of death—for after all, the most terrifying shadow is our own demise.

Thus in order to confront this particular shadow, we must stop, re-enter our bodies, and contemplate the reality of our personal, inexorable death. In the foreword to *Extinction Dialogs: How To Live With Death In Mind*, authored by myself and by Dr. Guy McPherson in 2014, Andrew Harvey states:

> *What the now-likely scenario of extinction is demanding of all of us is a going-beyond our human fantasies of entitlement, success and survival into a radical embodiment of what I would call the divine truth of our nondual identity – a truth that will be all the more inspiring and empowering in a situation when it alone can provide strength calm and continuing purpose.*[60]

The possibility of extinction, appearing more likely with each new scientific study of climate change, is first and foremost a momentous, cacophonous alarm, summoning us to radically abandon business as usual and allow ourselves to descend emotionally and spiritually into the deeper layers of the human psyche. We must abandon the American Dream and all other chimeras that promise that we can experience infinite growth on a finite planet. Our living arrangements and the entitlement underlying them must be dramatically altered. Do we open to this "radical embodiment" because it will save the planet? No indeed, because we have no guarantee that anything at this point can spare it.

Rather, we may choose the path of paradox and what

Jung called "holding the tension of opposites." From my perspective, this is the most "radical embodiment" of all. We alter our perception that saving the planet depends on us, or that anything we do or do not do will manifest the "death row" miracle so hoped for by the condemned inmate. We consume less, not because it will lower greenhouse gases, but because we need less, and it feels better to live more simply and perhaps express more generosity to others who have less. We seek avenues for sharing our love, and we allow our hearts to be broken open with compassion. Kindness, not entitlement, becomes our most cherished pre-occupation. We savor every occurrence of beauty and blessing in our lives, and we seek to create beauty in every circumstance. We treat other species with exquisite mercy and make their extinction as gentle as possible. Gratitude, not acquisition, becomes the motivating force of our lives. Moreover, we immerse ourselves in these practices, even as we witness the withering and perhaps irreversible departure of ecosystems. We allow beauty and sorrow to intersect in the flaming crucible of our hearts. We do all of this, not because our actions will somehow reverse abrupt, catastrophic climate change, but because doing so transports us to the core of our humanity and allows us to revel in the love and beauty of other beings.

Meanwhile, we allow ourselves to consciously grieve every personal and planetary loss of which we are aware because grief surgically opens our hearts and radically connects us with the Earth community—with all living beings, including ourselves.

If this sounds a bit like the attitude of the trained hospice worker, that's because it is. In his marvelous article

"The Planetary Hospice Movement," hospice worker, environmental activist and attorney Zhiwa Woodbury writes:

> Hospice is a subset of palliative care, and the concern of the Planetary Hospice Movement is itself palliative. To 'palliate' means "to lessen the severity of (pain, disease, etc.) without curing… [to] alleviate; mitigate." It doesn't mean that palliative care is incompatible with a course of treatment that may lead to a cure; rather, it is the physical, psychological, and spiritual suffering that is of concern to the palliative care team. That is the nature of the spiritual container for the Planetary Hospice Movement as well. It is concerned neither with saving nor condemning the world during this time of great dying and grieving. Instead, its over-riding, if not sole, concern is to alleviate the suffering attended with these most unfortunate times.[61]

Woodbury echoes the Mark Nepo quote that prefaces this chapter. Perhaps the noblest private act is the unheralded effort to return: to open our hearts once they've closed, to open our souls once they've shied away, to soften our minds once they've been hardened by the storms of our day.

We heal the shadow that extinction casts over our lives and relationships by keeping our hearts as open as possible and living as if each day—perhaps each moment —were the last. "There is nobody walking this earth who has not had their heart broken," says Woodbury. "If we develop the spiritual container to carry that broken heart around in our life, to keep it fresh without feeling like a victim, to own up to our pain, then it becomes an amazing, inexhaustible source of compassion, nourishment, and even joy....The point of getting in touch with our broken heart, or even picking the scab off an improperly healed heart, is not to finally heal it or even find closure. Rather, it is to learn to live in a state of constant healing, knowing that we can never be whole. That is a hard spiritual pill for some people to swallow."[62]

In a later chapter, we will explore the shadow invariably present in all activism, but in terms of the shadow of extinction, it is important to hold the tension of opposites: to pursue the forms of activism which resonate with our hearts, while at the same time bearing witness to all that is dissolving—including our own bodies.

Living as if we were in hospice and being hospice workers for all other beings means fundamentally returning to living life in the manner we were designed to live it. At the core of confronting the shadow of extinction must be our willingness to become mature men and women who fully recognize that death is a part of life, and that what gives our lives most meaning is love. For as Andrew Harvey notes:

> *Action is always the best antidote to despair, even when it cannot change the circumstances; action from a sacred consciousness is the one way in which even if we have to die out we can do so with dignity and without forfeiting the one thing we can still preserve—the essential beauty of our human divine truth.*[63]

— — — — — — — — — — — —

SUGGESTED PRACTICES: I frequently encounter individuals who wish to debate the issue of whether Earth and the human species "are going to make it" or not. Obviously, no one knows the answer to this question, nor do we actually know what "make it" looks like. My response to this debate is simply to state that I do not know if the planet or the human species will survive, but that that is less important than how we live in this moment.

Buddhist meditation instructor Ronya Banks lists a number of questions we should consider as we contemplate death, *but also as we contemplate living a meaningful life*:

How prepared am I to die?
What REALLY matters most to me? Have I led a meaningful life?
Have I loved well, with an open and generous heart? Is the world a better place because I was here?
How present have I been for each moment of my life?[64]

One of the most powerful practices for living under the shadow of death and confronting one's own fear of death is the practice of conscious grieving. Paradoxically, conscious grieving exquisitely prepares us to address each of the issues noted by Banks. Additionally, conscious grieving enhances our capacity to experience joy and appreciate beauty.

Highly recommended is the book The Wild Edge Of Sorrow by Francis Weller (2015). I consider Francis Weller the foremost expert on grief in the United States, and the reader may also wish to view his video on grief at: https://www.youtube.com/watch?v=EaI-4c92Mqo.

CHAPTER 8

COUNTERFEIT CULTURE

CONSUMERISM, EXCEPTIONALISM, NARCISSISM, AND ENTITLEMENT

Everything that everyone is afraid of has already happened: The fragility of capitalism, which we don't want to admit; the loss of the empire of the United States; and American exceptionalism. In fact, American exceptionalism is that we are exceptionally backward in about fifteen different categories, from education to infrastructure. But we're in a stage of denial: we want to re-establish things as they used to be, to put the country back where it was.

—James Hillman, Interview with James Hillman, Huffington Post, February 26, 2011 http://www.huffingtonpost. com/pythia- peay/america-and-the-shift-in- b 822913.html

In a 2014 Science Magazine article entitled "People Would Rather Be Electrically Shocked than Left Alone with Their Thoughts," Nadia Whitehead reports on a study at the

University of Virginia in which the participants were so uncomfortable with sitting and thinking, without external stimulation, that 67% of men and 25% of women chose to inflict electric shocks upon themselves rather than "just sit there quietly and think." Jonathan Schooler, a psychology professor at the University of California at Santa Barbara who studies consciousness, commented on the study, stating: "I found it quite surprising and a bit disheartening that people seem to be so uncomfortable when left to their own devices; that they can be so bored that even being shocked seemed more entertaining."[65]

While it is not news that the culture of industrial civilization is remarkably extroverted, a study such as the one above reveals that we have become something far beyond merely extroverted. We are so terrified of self- reflection that we prefer to inflict pain upon ourselves rather than engage with the inner world. While this finding reinforces the theory that industrial civilization fosters attraction to bizarre forms of stimulation such as exceedingly violent movies and extreme sports, it also reveals how little tolerance we have for introspection.

The shadow is alive and well in the collective and in everyone's external life, but substantial "intelligence gathering" regarding its machinations, as well as the capacity to tolerate the discomfort of consciously working with it, must begin in the inner world. When cultures are bereft of knowledge of the shadow and its transformation, they will invariably develop societies of self-absorption. The shadow will retreat further underground (into the unconscious) and be projected outward as "the Other" or that which is "not me." Contemplation and confrontation of the shadow produces mature men and women. Denial and repression of the shadow results in adolescent psyches that spawn vapid, superficial cultures that do not fulfill the over-arching purpose of culture. Their toxic influence precludes the creation of societies that achieve one of the primary functions of culture: to bond individuals and foster community. Consequently, until these shadow elements are healed, humans under their spell are only capable of creating myriad forms of misery within all socio-economic levels of society and perpetuating a fundamental belief in their separation from the Earth community and each other.

NARCISSISM IN THE AGE OF THE 'SELFIE'

If "bonding individuals and fostering community" is one of the explicit goals of culture, the milieu of industrial civilization has failed miserably. From the moment of conception, children of the middle class and the ruling elite are steeped in the fundamental tenet of their existence in this culture: narcissism. The implicit and explicit message is *You are special*. I do not wish to devalue the uniqueness of every child. In fact, narcissism obscures the individuality of each child by failing to notice that every child brings into the world unique gifts—gifts that are meaningless unless they are shared with the community. *You are special is synonymous with you are separate from and actually better than your peers*. Thus, the child's life begins with subtle but increasingly blatant indoctrination in "Othering." At worst, this inculcates sociopathy—others need to follow the rules, but I don't because I'm special. At best, the cult of specialness excludes the child from the human condition;

i.e., Other people get cancer, but I don't because I'm special; other people go bankrupt, but I don't because I'm special; other people's children have addiction issues, but you won't because you're special.

A recent phenomenon in our culture is the "selfie." Suddenly, we are a culture increasingly obsessed with taking pictures of ourselves. The reader may argue that I'm being over-analytical of the "harmless" selfie. Yet according to a recent Ohio State University study:

> ... *men who posted more photos of themselves online scored higher in measures of narcissism and psychopathy. The researchers asked 800 men between the ages of 18 and 40 to fill out an online questionnaire asking about their photo posting habits on social media. The survey included questions about how often they posted photos of themselves on social media, and about whether and how they edited photos before posting. The participants were also asked to fill out standard questionnaires measuring anti-social behaviors and self-objectification (the tendency to overly focus on one's appearance).*[66]

Throughout history, people have been enamored with self-portraits created in a variety of mediums, so what makes the selfie of the twenty-first century different? Furthermore, psychologists or social scientists might argue that because we lack low self-esteem, we have become obsessed with selfies. While both arguments are valid, I am fascinated with pre-occupation with the selfie in what is perhaps the most narcissistic culture in the history of our species. In fact, as a culture, we are self- obsessed, and the selfie is only one telling manifestation of that reality. Additionally telling is narcissism's next logical step.

ENTITLEMENT ON A PLANET OF SEVEN BILLION

If I am special (which actually means superior), this separates me from other humans and excludes me from many facets of the human condition. My specialness entitles me to bypass adversity at best and suffering at worst. Entitlement means that one has a right to something or is owed something by another person or entity—an attitude that invariably follows from the inculcation of specialness.

Both specialness and entitlement flourish in the soil of separation, and separation fosters self-interest. Inherent in specialness and entitlement is the notion that my self-interest can only advance at the expense of yours. When the entitled person hears statistics, such as nearly half the world's population, 2.8 billion people, survive on less than $2 a day; about 20 percent of the world's population, 1.2 billion people, live on less than $1 a day; nearly 1 billion people are illiterate and 1 billion do not have safe water, they may have little or no visceral or emotional response.[67] While we consciously understand that these statistics and the human beings they apply to are tragic, we also know, even if we don't understand the entire global framework of the statistics, that we are able to maintain our industrially civilized living arrangements as a result of the deplorable living arrangements of half of the world's population.

Most industrially civilized countries have created social safety nets such as food stamps, Social Security, Medicare, and other programs, which have been labeled "entitlements." Originally, these programs were put in place because societies believed that their more vulnerable members were 'entitled' to certain rights as a result of social equality or enfranchisement. Yet in recent decades, the ruling elite in our culture, giddy with a world view based on their own sense of entitlement, are moving rapidly and rapaciously to destroy all safety nets. Projecting their own sense of entitlement onto individuals who desperately need safety nets and accusing *them* of feeling entitled is a classic example of the pot calling the kettle black.

Entitlement is subtle and insidious. No one reading these words, nor the person writing them, escapes its far- reaching tentacles. While we may be keenly aware of our sense of entitlement in several areas, we may have blind spots in other areas. I have discovered that a profoundly effective medicine for the disease of entitlement is commitment to service in the world. A plethora of opportunities call to us: Teaching in jails or prisons, working with the homeless, volunteering in a hospice facility, fostering animals, mentoring at-risk youth, providing services for the developmentally disabled, visiting patients in nursing homes or assisted living facilities—the list is infinite. Each opportunity must be approached not only with an open heart, but with a willingness for the experience to stir one's own shadow material. When our compassion is activated, the shadow may be as well, and we may be taken aback by what mirrors are mobilized in the process of service. Therefore, we must approach opportunities to serve with an innocent openness to shadow instruction, which, if we are willing to endure it, will ultimately prove that the person most profoundly served is not the person we appear to be serving, but rather, ourselves.

EXCEPTIONALISM IS A TWO-WAY STREET

One frequently hears the term "American exceptionalism," which refers to the assumption that the United States is qualitatively different from other nations because it is morally superior. The notion originated with the Puritans, who declared that America was a "city set on a hill," and "a light unto the world," or a "New Jerusalem" which offered to the world a beacon of moral purity. Volumes have been written about the shadow of this Puritan assumption and how morally *im*-pure the Puritans were in terms of their relationships with native populations, their attitudes toward women, and their intolerance for world views other than their own. Nevertheless, the notion of exceptionalism lingers in the American psyche, adeptly facilitated and manipulated by politicians invested in winning wars and controlling public opinion—and by corporate capitalism whose agenda is the "sanctity" of consumerism.

But exceptionalism based on moral purity has been eclipsed by exceptionalism based on military might. As the late historian Howard Zinn wrote in a 2005 article entitled "The Power and The Glory: The Myths of American Exceptionalism":

> *One of the consequences of American exceptionalism is that the US government considers itself exempt from legal and moral standards accepted by other nations in the world.*

There is a long list of such self-exemptions: the refusal to sign the Kyoto Treaty regulating the pollution of the environment, the refusal to strengthen the convention on biological weapons. The United States has failed to join the hundred-plus nations that have agreed to ban land mines, in spite of the appalling statistics about amputations performed on children mutilated by those mines. It refuses to ban the use of napalm and cluster bombs. It insists that it must not be subject, as are other countries, to the jurisdiction of the International Criminal Court.

What is the answer to the insistence on American exceptionalism? Those of us in the United States and in the world who do not accept it must declare forcibly that the ethical norms concerning peace and human rights should be observed. It should be understood that the children of Iraq, of China, and of Africa, children everywhere in the world, have the same right to life as American children.[68]

While many Americans, and particularly American politicians, are eager to champion America's 'exceptional' moral purity and military might, few are willing to name the disgraceful ways in which the United States is exceptional. There are more people incarcerated in the US than in any other nation; there is a lingering racial divide spanning nearly four centuries; and America is the nucleus of international capitalism and the military- industrial-security complex. Moreover, let us not forget that the United States is the only nation that has ever attacked another country using nuclear weapons.

Domestically, white Americans rarely consider their privileged position in society. Many affirm that they hardly ever think about race, but in reality, they simply do not need to. In fact, if one is fortunate to have shelter, make a living wage, remain reasonably physically and mentally healthy, and have access to healthcare, education, clean water, and nutritious food, it is quite easy to succumb to the illusion of exceptionalism. For this reason, commitment to serving populations that do not have many or all of these advantages is perhaps the most effective medicine for healing the illusion. Whenever human beings are able to forget the reality that "there but for the grace of something greater go I," they are walking on ground that becomes fertile for the myth of exceptionalism. Heartfelt human connection with those for whom privilege is not an option offers its own cure for narcissism, entitlement, and exceptionalism.

RADICAL EMPATHY

It may be that the antidote to narcissism and entitlement is radical empathy which means the capacity to simply say, "I know how you feel" and mean it. More specifically, examples of radical empathy are offered by social change author Roman Krznaric in his book Empathy: Why It Matters And How To Get It. In the book, Krznaric notes the Six Habits Of Highly Empathic People, which I have listed below.[69] These simple but powerful practices not only impact the person practicing them, but enable profound social transformation.

- Cultivate curiosity about strangers. Specifically, according to Krznaric, "Cultivating curiosity requires more than having a brief chat about the weather. Crucially, it tries to understand the world inside the head of the other person. We are confronted by strangers every day, like the heavily tattooed woman who delivers your mail or the new employee who always eats his lunch alone. Set yourself the challenge of having a conversation with one stranger every week. All it requires is courage."

- Challenge prejudices and discover commonalities. As we pay attention to our tendencies to "Other" those of different ethnicities, cultures, religions, classes, and sexual orientations—as we work with the shadow aspects of Othering in our own psyches— commonalities become more obvious and empathy more heartfelt.

- Try another person's life. Accompanying another person in their daily routine or simply observing it closely evokes empathy, as well as many emotions which we may not be aware we are warding off when we resist closely observing their life.

- Listen hard and open up. Highly empathic people listen intently to other people. They not only listen, but remain present to the person to whom they are listening—and also present to what is going on inside of themselves as they listen. However, "Listening is never enough," says Krznaric. "The second trait is to make ourselves vulnerable. Removing our masks and revealing our feelings to someone is vital for creating a strong empathic bond. Empathy is a two-way street that, at its best, is built upon mutual understanding— an exchange of our most important beliefs and experiences."

- Inspire mass action and social change through empathy. Organize, write, protest, and use social networking to effect change, but just as important as spreading information and inspiration are empathic connections.
- Develop an ambitious imagination. It's easy to empathize with our allies, but the acid test is: Can we empathize with our adversaries? Or can we at least see the fear that lies under the oil company CEO's denial of global warming? Can we detect the panic on the face of the fundamentalist Christian minister who denounces gay marriage and the lifestyles of LGBT people? During the conflicts between Muslims and Hindus leading up to Indian independence in 1947, Gandhi declared, "I am a Muslim! And a Hindu, and a Christian and a Jew."[70]

CONSUMERISM VS. COMPOSTING

A culture engulfed in narcissism, entitlement, and exceptionalism, obsessed as it is with externalities, is a culture of inner emptiness. These shadows spawn hungry individuals who have created for themselves food deserts and "empty calorie" delicacies associated with diabetes, cancer, heart disease, and obesity. In what Canadian psychiatrist, Gabor Matè, calls "The Realm of The Hungry Ghosts," addiction has become rampant and in many instances, commonplace.[71]

In a milieu of externality, children do not discover the

treasures of an inner world which education (*educare*: to lead out) was originally designed to cultivate. Reflection and critical thinking are pre-empted by orgies of technology and elementary school television shopping channels. Few American children can find Alabama on the map of their nation, and "news" is an insipid concoction of entertainment and advertising. Civilized cultures do not foster face-to-face conversations between individuals or groups. Texting, emailing, and perpetual phone-staring have obliterated eye contact and attentive listening to another human being. The consumeristic culture's mantra is "more," and its official slogan is "now."

We should not then be surprised that in this "hungry ghost" culture of hyper-externality, we are encouraged to focus on the lives of celebrities and the latest episodes of reality television shows. Obsession with celebrities serves a number of purposes for the hungry ghosts. On the one hand, celebrities reinforce the American Dream mystique in a time when industrial growth societies are collapsing and financial meltdown or the specter of it is haunting collective consciousness. One day a waitress living on tips and a meager salary auditions for a role in a movie or appears on a television program such as The Voice, and overnight she is a star living in the lap of luxury where her only struggle is the avoidance of paparazzi. Psychologically, we live vicariously through our celebrities, witnessing their beauty, charisma, and talent, wishing it were our own yet "knowing" it will never be, and being willing to accept the consolation prize of envy from afar. Hence the Golden Shadow named by Andrew Harvey in Chapter 1 of this book, which is a projection externally onto a venerated human being, thereby minimizing or even disowning the same admirable qualities in oneself.

Our voracious, insatiable hunger for community drives us to movies and TV series that engulf us in dramas and hypothetical predicaments, offering cheap substitutes for meaningful contact with other human beings. We may converse about these in person with friends or in the comment section of a blog online, but in the end, we remain isolated and alone. The emptiness persists.

Addictions beckon, and we attempt to alleviate the emptiness with substances, sexuality, food, or a host of compulsive behaviors. When all else fails, or perhaps even the instant we feel the void, we go shopping. Many women who have accumulated massive credit card debt and teeter on the edge of bankruptcy admit that shopping temporarily fills the emptiness. They may have one hundred pair of shoes, but they believe that one more pair will make the emptiness go away. Often they carry out the shopping ritual, realize the error of their binge, and return the merchandise the following day because filling the emptiness in the moment was more important than keeping what they bought. Stories of shopaholic sprees and the individuals involved are regularly featured on television shows hosted by financial gurus such as Suze Orman, or on Gail Vaz Oxlade's award-winning Canadian TV program "'Til Debt Do Us Part."

Consumer culture is watered and fertilized by narcissism, entitlement, and exceptionalism—the shadows of the American Dream and the "good life." In order to heal these shadows, they must be faced squarely and decisively. The doorway to the healing process is to consciously sit with the emptiness. One may journal about the experience of emptiness, ask the unconscious mind for dreams on the theme, and creatively construct other options for filling the vacuum. However, eventually, the feeling of emptiness must be felt and metabolized.

Yet even as we open to emptiness, we have the option of approaching life, indeed all of creation, with an attitude of reverence. As Francis Weller writes, "Reverence, rather than expectation or entitlement, acknowledges we live in a gifting cosmos and that we do best honoring creation by singing praises. As the poet Rilke said, 'To praise is the whole thing! A man who can praise comes toward us like ore out of the silences of rock.' Reverence acknowledges that what we are seeing or seeking is holy; that we depend utterly on this world to breathe and to dream."[72]

In a chapter entitled "The Flute of Interior Time" from his 2014 book *The Endless Practice: Becoming Who You Were Born To Be*, Mark Nepo writes:

> *In truth, we fill ourselves up to avoid our conversation with death, though the vastness that holds even death opens us to a greater understanding of life. This is the beginning of depth experience, which getting close to, we often run from, quickly trying to fill ourselves up again…Paradoxically, it's the emptiness of things that lets us glimpse their full capacity. Most musical instruments are hollowed out, because if they weren't, there would be no music. Guitars are hollowed out. String instruments are hollowed out. This is a great example of the necessity of emptiness in order to make music. It's true with our lives. Each of us is an instrument that*

experience hollows out in order to have our souls release their song.[73]

The ultimate antidote to consumerism is the practice of composting, both literally and symbolically. When we attend to what we can give—how our love, compassion, attention, and the gifts we came here to share can enrich the landscape of barren places and barren people—we discover within our own emptiness and that of others an unprecedented whole-heartedness, a quality of aliveness of which counterfeit culture is bereft. The consummate lie of counterfeit culture is that happiness issues from narcissism, entitlement, and exceptionalism. On the other hand, a culture is made whole when consumerism is supplanted by gift; when exceptionalism is redefined by union; when narcissism surrenders to interdependence; and when entitlement is transformed by sharing.

— — — — — — — — — — —

SUGGESTED PRACTICES: Sadly, attitudes of entitlement in a culture of exceptionalism and privilege become as natural as breathing air, and all inhabitants of industrial civilization carry some traces of it. The fundamental assumption in this milieu is that we are separate from each other and the Earth community. The delusion of separation engenders a host of other delusions, such as the notion that suffering is unnatural and unfair. These assumptions result in the notion that we are special and should not have to suffer or even be inconvenienced. Thus, the work of all spiritual seekers must be the journey from entitlement to empathy.

Anything we can do to heal our belief in separation will automatically diminish a sense of entitlement. When we not only understand but experience that we are interconnected with all living beings, our capacity to be empathic expands exponentially.

PRACTICES FOR TRANSFORMING ENTITLEMENT

1. *Tonglen.* A number of meditation practices facilitate the healing of a belief in separation as well as a deepening of empathy. One practice particularly useful is the Tibetan Buddhist practice of *tonglen.* Tibetan Buddhist teacher Pema Chodron explains *tonglen* as follows:

    On the in-breath, you breathe in whatever particular area, group of people, country, or even one particular person – maybe it's not this more global situation, maybe it's breathing in the physical discomfort and mental anguish of chemotherapy; of all the people who are undergoing chemotherapy. And if you've undergone chemotherapy and come out the other side, it's very real to you. Or maybe it's the pain of those who have lost loved ones – suddenly, or recently, unexpectedly or over a long period of time, some dying. But the in-breath is – you find some place on the planet in your personal life or something you know about, and you breathe in with the wish that those human beings or those mistreated animals or whoever it is, that they could be free of that suffering, and you breathe in with the longing to remove their suffering.

    And then you send out – just relax out – send

enough space so that peoples' hearts and minds feel big enough to live with their discomfort, their fear, their anger or their despair, or their physical or mental anguish. But you can also breathe out for those who have no food and drink, you can breathe out food and drink. For those who are homeless, you can breathe out/send them shelter. For those who are suffering in any way, you can send out safety, comfort.

So in the in-breath you breathe in with the wish to take away the suffering, and breathe out with the wish to send comfort and happiness to the same people, animals, nations, or whatever it is you decide.

Do this for an individual, or do this for large areas, and if you do this with more than one subject in mind, that's fine… breathing in as fully as you can, radiating out as widely as you can.

A more detailed explanation of Tonglen is given by Pema Chodron in a You Tube video entitled "Tonglen Meditation."(www.youtube.com/watch?v=QwqlurCvXuM)

See also www.en.wikipedia.org/wiki/Tonglen.

2) Service. From the entitlement perspective, we "shouldn't have to suffer" and must avoid it at all costs because it disturbs our happiness. In the modern world we have come to believe that suffering and happiness are polar opposites. What all wisdom traditions teach, however, is that suffering and happiness are inextricably connected,

or as Buddhist teacher Thich Nhat Hanh writes, "...the art of happiness is also the art of suffering well. When we learn to acknowledge, embrace, and understand our suffering, we suffer much less. Not only that, but we're also able to go further and transform our suffering into understanding, compassion, and joy for ourselves and for others."

Anything we can do to cultivate empathy and compassion within ourselves will transform our sense of entitlement. Moving out of our comfort zone to serve other suffering beings is essential. Thus, it is imperative that we follow the calling of our hearts to service in the world. Service may involve a formal occupation, or it may be offered on a volunteer basis. In a shattered and battered world, a plethora of opportunities to serve await our willingness to step into them. One cannot inhabit the domain of entitlement while rendering honest, empathic service. Commit to one practice of regular service in your community, as well as offering smaller acts of service daily.

3. Gratitude. Inextricably connected with tonglen and service is gratitude. Just as it is impossible to feel entitled when we are experiencing empathy, it is impossible to feel entitled when we are practicing gratitude. As David Stendl-Rast writes in *Gratefulness, The Heart of Prayer: An Approach To Life In Fullness*, "Gratefulness always goes beyond myself. For what makes something a gift is precisely that it is given. And the receiver depends on the

giver.[74] When we feel entitled, we are marooned on the island of "it's all about me." When we are grateful, something in us recognizes our interdependence, our vulnerability to the human condition, and the precariousness of our exceptionalism. Rather than taking our lives "for granted," says Stendl-Rast, in practicing gratitude, we realize that everything in our lives, including life itself, has been "granted" to us.[75]

4) Presence. Just as it is impossible to feel entitled when practicing gratitude, it is impossible to feel entitled when practicing being present. Entitlement is never about fully attending to the present moment. The entitled perspective focuses incessantly on the future, particularly on how we will be perceived by others and how we will maintain a perpetual state of happiness. From that perspective, one is never fully present in the moment, but obsessively planning for future comfort and control. Entitlement spawns anxiety, obsessive-compulsive behavior, and unrelenting posturing in order to defend one's entitled status. Thus when we practice being present in the moment, we distance ourselves from pre-occupation with future outcomes, and we invariably become more present in the body, as well as present and available for others.

Using the breath to become present is key. In No Mud, No Lotus, Thich Nhat Hanh offers 16 powerful breathing exercises for helping us abide in the present moment.

Eckhart Tolle famously suggests that when engaged in any activity, we frequently check in with ourselves to notice if we are still breathing. And, when we engage in any activity, he suggests that we engage with great attentiveness. For example, when washing the dishes, smell the soap, feel the temperature of the water on the hands, carefully observe the cup or plate being washed, notice how mundane the activity may feel, notice the breath—and when the mind wanders to future activities, bring the attention back to the present moment.

Tonglen, service, practicing gratitude, and being present are unerring elixirs for transforming entitlement.

CHAPTER 9

THE ACTIVIST AND THE SHADOW

THE FIRES OF TRIUMPHALISM AND THE WATERS OF GRIEF

> *Do not depend on the hope of results....You may have to face the fact that your work will be apparently worthless and even achieve no result at all, if not perhaps results opposite to what you expect. As you get used to this idea, you start more and more to concentrate not on the results, but on the value, the rightness, the truth of the work itself.*
>
> **—Thomas Merton, The Hidden Ground Of Love**

In his book Endgame, Volume I, activist Derrick Jensen shares a brief but profound story:

> *A while back I got an email from someone in Spokane, Washington. He said his fifteen-year-old son was wonderfully active in the struggle for ecological and social sanity. But, the father continued, "I want to make sure he stays active, so I feel the need to give him hope. This is a problem,*

> *because I don't feel any hope myself, and I don't*
> *want to lie to him." I told him not to lie and said*
> *if he wants his son to stay active, he shouldn't try to*
> *give him hope, but instead to GIVE HIM LOVE.*
> *If his son learns how to love, he will stay active.*[76]

As the shadow of human extinction hovers, whether it occurs this century or millennia from now or never, we presently hear a cacophony of individuals who are aware of our predicament yet champion the notion of *hope*. We dare not give up hope, they say, because where there is life, there is hope. At the slightest suggestion that what we are confronting is so enormous that it spells our unequivocal demise, these voices argue that abandoning hope is the same as giving up.

I suggest that two alternatives are preferable to "hoping." The first, of course, is action, and clearly, activists *act*. However, I further suggest that hope should not be the ultimate motivation for acting. When we take action as a result of hope, we are more vulnerable to burnout and what has become known in recent years as "compassion fatigue." What if instead of acting on the basis of hope, we act because we feel drawn to a particular cause, knowing that it is the right thing to do or because we feel unable to do otherwise? What if our passion alone and the satisfaction we receive in taking action compel us to persevere? What if we knew with certainty that our efforts would make absolutely no difference long-term, but we felt we could not do otherwise? What if we act for the sake of acting?

Hope is vague, amorphous, and exceedingly vulnerable to the frailties of doubt. Passionately doing what is right *because* it is right transports us beyond the capriciousness of hope and into spiritual practice. Many activists who consistently act from this sort of motivation would not name it a spiritual practice, but in fact, it is. Activism motivated by a commitment to peace, empathy, compassion, the alleviation of suffering, community building, intimacy with the earth, and crafting authentic communication is behavior aligned with the principles of all of the great wisdom traditions. In the words of Buddhist teacher and activist Bernie Glassman:

> *When we bear witness, when we become the situation—homelessness, poverty, illness, violence, death—the right action arises by itself. We don't have to worry about what to do. We don't have to figure out solutions ahead of time. Peacemaking is the functioning of bearing witness. Once we listen with our entire body and mind, loving action arises.*

> *Loving action is right action. It's as simple as giving a hand to someone who stumbles or picking up a child who has fallen on the floor. We take such direct, natural actions every day of our lives without considering them special. And they're not special. Each is simply the best possible response to that situation in that moment.*[77]

Spiritual traditions teach that bearing witness is an act that not only affects the person or situation being observed, but the observer as well. In my experience, when I am able to be fully present to the situation in which I am engaged as an activist, all of the trappings of hope recede into the background of my consciousness, and I am absorbed in the current moment of action.

We are not called to save the world, but rather, to act with love—or more specifically, to be love in action. Being love in action means that we are not seduced by one of activism's most deceptive shadows: success. As Andrew Harvey, author of *The Hope: A Guide to Sacred Activism*, writes, "Beyond hope lies Love, Love for its own sake and truth and radiance, Love that we must learn to embody and act out on every level in every way to find meaning and joy in the final situation we have created from our ignorance and greed."[78]

Rather than becoming engulfed in notions of success or failure, we must face the limits of human agency and the glory of surrender. But what *is* surrender, and how is it different from giving up? Is "surrender" another word for defeatism? One benchmark for discerning the difference can be found in the world of archetypes.

Human consciousness is deeply influenced by personal and cultural archetypes—universal themes of which we may or may not be aware. Here are just a few examples of archetypes: *mother, father, hero, savior, martyr, warrior, maiden, crone, healer,* and more. If we are not aware of the archetypes that influence us, we may unconsciously live them out in both creative and destructive ways.

Mythologist Joseph Campbell wrote and taught more about the hero archetype than perhaps anyone in modern times. Campbell simply defined the hero/heroine as "someone who has given his or her life to something bigger than oneself." According to Campbell, the hero's journey is threefold: separation, initiation, and return. He/ she usually experiences some sort of unusual circumstances at birth; sustains a traumatic wound; acquires a special weapon that only he/she can use; and proves him/herself by way of some sort of quest or journey through which he/she is forever changed. The hero's journey is one of death, rebirth, and transformation on which he/she embarks for the wellbeing of the community. Meanwhile, it is the hero, as well as the community, who is transformed.

The pitfalls along the journey are many, but one of the most common—and also the most injurious to the hero and the community—is to become inflated with one's heroic mission. One's passionate commitment to the journey makes avoidance of this particular snare exceedingly difficult. Along the way, the hero may find him/herself becoming inflated, but can always choose to pause, reflecting on the purpose of the journey and the "something bigger" which compelled the hero to set out in the first place. This reflection is an opportunity to surrender to the ultimate purpose of the journey and the spiritual forces that motivated and support the hero. *In all of mythology, the ultimate purpose is the transformation of consciousness, both one's own and that of the community. Moreover, in mythology, failure to surrender to the larger purpose of the journey guarantees the hero's demise.*

In Greek mythology the hero was always aware of the seduction of thinking himself equal to or wiser than the gods. Whenever heroes succumbed to this temptation, they began plummeting toward their demise. Perhaps the most famous example of the inflated hero is Icarus, who in his determination to soar flew too close to the sun, whereby his wings, which were made of wax, began melting, and he fell into the sea. Whether the wax wings of Icarus or the vulnerable heel of Achilles, the fundamental lesson with which all Greek mythological heroes were confronted was their human limitations and the consequences of forgetting those.

The hero symbolizes courage and sometimes appears as a warrior as well, but whether hero or warrior, courage is one of his/her stellar characteristics. One lesson the hero/warrior must learn is when to fight relentlessly and when to exercise restraint, and when to surrender, for whatever reason, to the dilemma with which he/she is confronted. The Shambhala Warrior, for example, receives training in fighting spiritual rather than physical battles. Discernment regarding restraint versus full-on combat is pivotal, and at all times the warrior must examine the heart and will. He/she does not continue fighting at all costs simply because "that is what warriors do." Rather, the spiritual warrior considers whether or not it is time to stop fighting altogether, or whether it may be time to change strategy. Fighting may not mean "winning" in the heroic sense, but rather may mean fighting for reasons that surpass even one's survival.

What we need now is not heroic victory but, in the words of Andrew Harvey, an "astringent maturity," an entirely new level of adulthood that acts in ways that bring forth optimum joy, optimum healing, and optimum beauty.

The sacred inspiration we require results not from false hope or finding solutions, but from a state of active being in which we voluntarily enroll in radical psychological and spiritual training. If we haven't enrolled in this psycho-spiritual apprenticeship, then we will persevere in our triumphalist agenda and inadvertently perpetuate despair. We must recognize that the magnitude of the global crisis exceeds anything humans have yet been forced to confront. For this reason, its gift, according to Harvey, is the gift of any initiatory experience: "the shattering of the ego and being forced to stop clinging to any false hope or anything except the Sacred Self— deathless love, deathless compassion, deathless courage, deathless service. In that process we find great peace, great love."[79]

In his 2015 article, "Activism in the New Story," Charles Eisenstein admonishes us to redefine our notions of "winners" and "losers." He emphasizes that when we are attached to being winners or losers, "…the outcome will be influenced by the playing out of psychological dramas, because the events of our lives unfold in reflection of our own shadows, fears, unresolved inner conflicts, and so on."[80] However, approaching our activism from a perspective of equanimity is daunting. How much easier to view ourselves as "righteous" and the opponent as "evil."

For this reason, of paramount importance in the new Sacred Activism is regular, conscious grief work. Unless activists mourn, they can easily be consumed with the fires of passion because their psyches are not tempered with the waters of grief. Conscious grieving is an integral aspect of the "astringent maturity" we develop as we balance hero/warrior courage with discerning acceptance of our predicament. In his marvelous book *The Wild Edge of Sorrow*, Francis Weller states:

> *Grief is the work of mature men and women. It is our responsibility to be available to this emotion and offer it back to our struggling world. The gift of grief is the affirmation of life and of our intimacy with the world. It is risky to stay open and vulnerable in a culture increasingly dedicated to death, but without our willingness to stand*

> *witness through the power of our grief, we will not be able to stem the hemorrhaging of our communities, the senseless destruction of ecologies or the basic tyranny of monotonous existence… Grief is…a powerful form of soul activism. If we refuse or neglect the responsibility for drinking the tears of the world, her losses and deaths cease to be registered by the ones meant to be the receptors of that information. It is our job to feel the losses and mourn them. It is our job to openly grieve for the loss of wetlands, the destruction of forest systems, the decay of whale populations, the erosion of soil, and on and on. We know the litany of loss, but we have collectively neglected our emotional response to this emptying of our world.*[81]

For hundreds of years, members of the Dagara Tribe of West Africa have practiced regular grief rituals because they believe that both the Earth and the community need periodic releases of grief. Without doing so, they say, the heart becomes and remains hard, and this becomes toxic for the community. Always a community versus a private ritual, the Dagara experience that grieving together solidifies the community and makes conflict resolution less problematic and complicated. As a result of the community grieving together, members of the tribe also experience something that Westerners might not expect; namely, a deepening of joy. In The Wild Edge of Sorrow, Francis Weller shares his conversation with a Dagara woman immediately following a grief ritual. The woman displayed a radiant smile and seemed to exude joy from every pore. When he asked her how she could be so happy after engaging in a grief ritual, she responded with something like, "I'm so happy because I cry all the time." Her response, it seems, echoes the profound words of William Blake: "The deeper the sorrow, the greater the joy."

Sacred Activist, author and educator Ann Amberg speaks of "partnering with loss."[82] Upon first reading those words, I was captivated by the phrase because indeed, that is the crux of the new Sacred Activism. In partnering with loss, we open a door to unfathomable intimacy with the universe—a relationship that has the capacity to profoundly alter our very identity as consciously self-aware humans. It is one thing to struggle to save the Earth, yet quite another matter to feel oneself inextricably connected with it in every cell of the body.

What is more, conscious grieving humbles us and entreats us to relinquish our pre-conceived agenda. The sacred self is expanded even as the ego contracts, and we are radically opened to organize in service of objectives far nobler and more strategic than those forged by reason alone.

Heroic activism, and particularly activism without grief work, invariably leads to burnout and compromised bodies and psyches. Self-care, including grieving, is not self-indulgent, but rather a spiritual practice that honors the corporeal container's permeation by the sacred for the purpose of advancing its work.

Only recently have some activists discovered that they cannot endure the fires of activism nor have a positive impact in the external world unless they are willing to commit to a journey of inner psycho-spiritual work. In fact, what we protest or endeavor to change in the outer landscape is a reflection of the inner world. Why are we drawn to one issue as opposed to another? In *The Hope: A Guide to*

Sacred Activism, Andrew Harvey counsels each reader to look inside themselves and feel into a particular social issue that literally breaks their heart, because that is the cause to which they must commit. In other words, follow the heartbreak. For example, what is it about homelessness that breaks your heart, or what is it about the abuse and neglect of animals that pierces your core?

Wisely, Andrew suggests following the heartbreak because to choose to become an activist on behalf of any cause that we do not feel passionately about is to avoid a deep inner wound and thereby commit half-heartedly. Many spiritual traditions teach that in the psyche, every person's gift lies in close proximity with their wound, and that the wounds we carry and the gifts we bring into the world need each other.

Commitment to a cause that breaks our hearts will evoke our wounds as well as the shadow. Thus, as we encounter injustice and the perpetrators of it, we are likely to observe ourselves behaving in the same way the perpetrator behaves. For example, on the very morning of the day on which I am writing these words, I was watching a news story on television about the anti-war group Code Pink protesting at the Senate Armed Services Committee in Washington. Code Pink attempted to perform a citizen's arrest of former Secretary of State Henry Kissinger when he arrived to testify on global security challenges at a Senate Armed Services Committee meeting. In response, Senator John McCain, Chairman of the Senate Armed Services Committee, shouted, "I've been a member of this committee for many years, and I have never seen anything as disgraceful and outrageous and despicable as the last demonstration that just took place …you know, you're going to have to shut up, or I'm going to have you arrested. … Get out of here, you low-life scum." At that moment, I felt violent rage surging throughout my body. I wanted to reach through the TV screen and strangle McCain. As I finished audibly cursing him soundly, I realized that I was displaying the same behavior as McCain. In the next moment, my body was filled with deep humiliation and shame as I realized the irrepressible presence and power of my shadow. Obviously, I have much more inner work to do. Time to return to the Victim/Tyrant/Savior/Rebel matrix and resume processing those dynamics in myself.

In his essay "What Is Action?" Charles Eisenstein emphasizes the necessity of inner work and interpersonal work:

> *Many activists are coming to believe that more of the same is not enough; that we need to act from a different place—and that requires inner work and interpersonal work. I think many common tactics used by environmentalists and political progressives are actually counterproductive—not because they are insufficiently clever, but because they encode some of the same deep worldview from which ecocide and oppression arise as well.*[83]

The activist committed to inner work as well as outer struggles for social and Earth justice will invariably discover that they cannot simply function as a spiritual practitioner or an activist, but that they must integrate their psycho-spiritual journey with their activist mission. As Jungian author Paul Levy notes, the wound is also the gift:

> *Our wound is initiatory in that it is literally*
> *prodding and prompting us to evolve into a freer,*
> *more coherent, and higher order of ourselves.*
> *Hidden in our wound is its own re-solution. This*
> *is to say that the wound itself is an expression*
> *of the part of us, which, to speak from outside*
> *of linear time for a moment, is already healed.*
> *An expression of the ground of being, our wound*
> *connects us to life itself. We don't cure our wound.*
> *It cures us.* [84]

Much of our shadow can be revealed and healed as we consciously participate in grief work. Often, activists do not grasp the connection between the fires of activism and the waters of grief, and how one needs the other. However, the one alchemical element present in resolving the disparity and integrating the two is the component of love. We struggle for justice from a vast well of love, and our grief issues from the same well. Rather than impairing our activism, grief revitalizes and empowers it, because in fact, to grieve is to love.

Love is not an emotion or a sentiment, but rather a state of being we can access at any time—from the pinnacle of passionate activism as well as in the yawning abyss of wrenching grief. Love in action is an expression of our infinite capacity flowing through the conduit of consciousness. As the late spiritual teacher Osho states:

> *I love, because my love is not dependent on the*
> *object of love. My love is dependent on my state*
> *of being. So whether the other person changes,*
> *becomes different, friend turns into a foe, does*
> *not matter, because my love was never dependent*

on the other person. My love is my state of being.
I simply love.[85]

Charles Eisenstein also speaks of the "invisible matrix of causality."[86] Because none of us is separate from anyone or anything in the universe, every act, whether deemed "positive" or "negative," has an effect on everything else in the universe. Our culture encourages us to believe that our actions are not significant unless they are calculable, measurable, and highly visible. Many activists assume that unless their efforts are dramatic and demonstrated on a massive scale, they aren't doing enough. While large-scale movements and conspicuous protests raise awareness and often alter the course of an entire culture, we cannot deny their appeal to the ego. Meanwhile, according to Eisenstein, for every big-name activist, there are hundreds of humble individuals holding society together with compassion and service. Is a mother taking care of a terminally ill child, or a person serving food to the homeless, or a small group of people rescuing dogs from a puppy mill doing something less important than an activist "rock star"? In the invisible matrix of causality, each one of these expressions of love is impacting all beings.

More simply, the invisible matrix of causality can be summarized by these words from poet and essayist Mark Nepo:

> *...when kind, we're not just helping the person*
> *before us but evolving the heart of humanity.*
> *Little by little, nurture can become nature. Every*
> *inch of kindness matters. A kindness earned can*

become inborn. This is the deepest education. One
that lives in our bones.[87]

— — — — — — — — — — — —

SUGGESTED PRACTICES: For the most part, activists are committed to examining root causes, and from that perspective, devising solutions that address the issues. Often they are called "radical," which to their opponents means extreme, unrealistic, or even violent. In fact, the word "radical" is related to "root," and the authentic radical is always focused on the root of whatever issue they are confronting.

It is challenging, but not impossible, to be an engaged activist without being attached to the solutions one considers the most appropriate. When the activist invests months, years, or decades in organizing around a particular cause only to witness their envisioned solutions abandoned or sabotaged, they may become bitter, cynical, despairing, depressed, and numb.

The shadow of engaged, open-hearted activism is an ego inflation that insists on a particular outcome. Unfortunately, it is all too easy to become ensnared by an implacable attachment to outcome, particularly when the opposition constantly seeks to co-opt or derail the activist's agenda.

Chapter 9 is written from the perspective of what Andrew Harvey calls the New Sacred Activism. Accordingly, the following reflections offer opportunities for healing the shadow as it may appear in our activist endeavors.

1) Describe your commitment to activism. What is the flame of passion that drives you to organize or campaign around a particular issue?

2) What is your ideal outcome in terms of your efforts?

3) How invested is your ego in this outcome? What will be your response(s) if you do not see the outcome you want?

4) What do you know about your own grief with respect to the issues in which you are involved as well as the state of the planet?

5) Do you allow yourself to consciously grieve about these issues? If you do not allow yourself to grieve, what prevents you from doing so? If you do allow yourself to grieve, what have been the results of doing so?

6. Highly recommended is Francis Weller's 2015 book *The Wild Edge of Sorrow*. It is a tender toolkit of nurturing support for conscious grieving.

7. Do you have a spiritual practice? If so, what role does it play in your activism? If you do not have a spiritual practice, are there other avenues available to you for making meaning and creating purpose in your life and activism?

CHAPTER 10

THE SHADOW OF NEW AGE SPIRITUALITY: VIOLENT FUNDAMENTALISM

Frankly, happiness is overrated. I like being happy. But it's a welcome mood and not the basis of a moral code. Happiness is one of a thousand feelings and under it, and all the other human feelings, is the depth of being alive.

—Mark Nepo, Endless Practice:BecomingWhoYouWere Born to Be

Spiritually speaking, you are only able to go as high as you are willing to go deep.

—Leslie Temple Thurston, Marriage of Spirit

In my early thirties I was on a mission—a mission to find the meaning of life and my place in it. Having grown up in a fundamentalist Christian family, subservient to an angry, vengeful God who demanded perfection and obedience, I had dramatically rebelled in my twenties. Indeed it was the era of drugs, sex, and rock and roll, and as with most inordinately repressed young people, much of my life was dedicated to shameless rebellion. In the mid-1970s as the hippie generation abandoned Haight- Ashbury and anti-war protests, settled into marriage and raising families, fled to ashrams (or in my case, graduate school) the trajectory of their energy became much less external and more self-focused.

My experiment with abject atheism metamorphosed into psychedelic exploration and a profound sense of something abiding within me that superseded reason or intellect. As a voracious reader I devoured what the rest of my generation was also taking in: Herman Hesse, Wolfgang Goethe, Theodore Roszak, Alan Watts, Aldous Huxley, Carlos Castaneda, and more. Meditation became an inherent part of my life as I gravitated increasingly toward Eastern spirituality and the study of consciousness. In the late seventies I moved from the Mountain West to Southern California. Suddenly, I was engulfed in a dizzying scenario of alternative spiritual options. I began attending Unity and Science of Mind churches and inhaling every book and tape recording on New Age spirituality. These fell like luscious rivulets of water on a soul parched and scorched by a Midwest hellfire and brimstone childhood.

Not only was I assured that the universe was entirely loving, positive, and benevolent, but if I could maintain a positive outlook and reject negative thinking in any form, I would be guaranteed a life of abundance, loving relationships, impeccable health, and all things incontrovertibly idyllic. Thirty years before Rhonda Byrne's blathering, nonsensical book and movie *The Secret*, I was ensconced in the illusion of "having it all."

In fact, I never *did* have it all, but nevertheless persisted in believing I could. My financial challenges were "only because" I wasn't thinking positively enough, and my disastrous track record with relationships was "only because" of my negative thinking.

At the age of 40, however, something both wonderful and horrific happened as my life fell apart. Clearly, my New Age spirituality wasn't working and in fact, had mobilized an assemblage of blind spots in my awareness. Desperate, I entered psychotherapy with a woman skillfully trained in Jungian depth therapy, and I commenced a journey that lasted more than a decade—a journey that both saved and permanently altered my life in ways I could have never imagined.

One of my first awarenesses on the journey was the reality of the human shadow and the sense of what mine looked like. Eventually, I came to understand that while my essence was and is sacred, many other parts of my psyche had incorporated the violence, paranoia, and hypocrisy of my upbringing, and no amount of positive thinking could erase these. Denying or evading this darkness was not an option. Rather, I needed to descend into these wounds because, as I quickly learned, the only way *out was through.* My eleven years on this journey were both tumultuous and glorious. Countless times I considered suicide or terminating therapy. But inexplicably, I returned and persevered. Yet not only did I discover the horrors of my personal shadow, but the beauty and delight of the bright shadow I had sent away very early in my life.

On the one hand, I could have remained in therapy another decade, but some part of me knew I needed to end a formal therapeutic process and live my new life in the world, fully aware that I would falter and fail and make both old and new mistakes in every aspect of my life. Today, from hindsight, I know that my choice to move beyond therapy was wise, even as my path unfolded erratically for the next fifteen years. Yet because of my commitment to confront and abide with the shadow, imperfect as it was, I am not only alive today but experiencing a fuller integration of the shadow in the psyche than I could have imagined. That journey is all that qualifies me to write these words, and without it, I might have recklessly destroyed myself and many in my path.

Enormously enticing for me in my experiment with New Age spirituality was the notion that suffering, evil, and the dark side of humanity are not real. From a darkness-phobic perspective, these are perceived as illusions, so that when confronting what "appears" as darkness or adversity, one must affirm the light and mentally cancel suggestions of anything but goodness or the presence of God. When becoming aware of one's own anger, fear, or sadness, one is advised to affirm that no other emotions than love are real. That is, when feeling anger, a student of New Age spirituality learns to affirm that they are only love and that no other emotion exists.

In other words, the devout practice of adhering only to positive thoughts and emotions is a massive, perpetual regimen of denial. Nothing is allowed in consciousness except light and love.

While basking in the sunlight of positive thinking was more pleasurable for me than allowing the presence of the so-called "negative," it neither rang true nor felt consistent with the full spectrum of my humanity. As I read the works of Jung and as I opened to the reality of my own personal shadow, on the one hand, I felt more emotional distress; but on the other, exploring the forbidden territory of my psyche felt profoundly authentic and substantial. I soon realized that New Age spirituality offered a dubious peace of mind at the expense of familiarity with my humanity and the human condition at large. In fact, I came to understand that addiction to positive thinking precariously ignores the dark side of humanity and in doing so, conceals the shadow of rigidity, judgmentalism, and self-righteous arrogance that lurks beneath the still waters of "living in the light." Specifically, while declaring itself liberated from the fundamentalist perspective, New Age spirituality is fertile ground for reactive zealotry—a virtual hothouse for the development of violent extremism, precisely because it is unwilling to engage the human shadow.

While I concur with the world's great wisdom traditions that admonish us not to judge anyone or anything, I have also experienced that it is crucial to be aware of the emotions lurking within us that arouse judgment. For example, the rantings of an ultra- conservative fundamentalist Christian politician frequently incites anger within me, and if I do not own the anger but stoically exhort myself not to judge without recognizing the anger and including it as one aspect of my response to the political diatribe, I may be setting myself up for a subsequent explosive outburst. Is it not wiser to feel my anger, perhaps even venting it privately on some inanimate object, and then process the emotion, allowing it to find its own place in my psyche—rather than to immediately externalize my reaction in an aggressive or hurtful manner? Is the former not a more authentic response?

Professor, author, and Episcopal priest Barbara Brown Taylor speaks of "full-on solar spirituality" which excludes the necessary darkness of human experience.[88] In a Time Magazine article "In Praise Of Darkness," she writes:

> *"Darkness" is shorthand for anything that scares me — that I want no part of — either because I am sure that I do not have the resources to survive it or because I do not want to find out. The absence of God is in there, along with the fear of dementia and the loss of those nearest and dearest to me. So is the melting of polar ice caps, the suffering of children, and the nagging question of what it will feel like to die. If I had my way, I would eliminate everything from chronic back pain to the fear of the devil from my life and the lives of those I love — if I could just find the right night-lights to leave on.*

> *At least I think I would. The problem is this: when, despite all my best efforts, the lights have gone off in my life (literally or figuratively, take your pick), plunging me into the kind of darkness that turns my knees to water, nonetheless I have not died. The monsters have not dragged me out of bed and taken me back to their lair. The witches have not turned me into a bat. Instead, I have learned things in the dark that I could never have learned in the light, things that have saved my life over and over again, so that there is really only one logical conclusion. I need darkness as much as I need light.*[89]

Beyond nurturing inauthenticity, the full-on-solar

perspective is inordinately self-centered and narcissistic, with a myopic focus on one's own personal evolution. One is encouraged to get on with their own liberation and the fulfillment of their own potential. To do otherwise is to "succumb" to negative thinking. While attention to one's personal spiritual evolution is crucial, myopic focus on it perpetuates the illusion of separation from the earth community and from what Rabbi Irwin Kula names "the sacred messiness of life."[90]

A term often frequently bandied about in New Age circles is "ascension," which is often synonymous with transcending the human condition. For some New Age groups, ascension literally means leaving the physical body and becoming only a spirit being. History is replete with cults and spiritual groups that have claimed the power to move beyond the physical body into purely spirit form.

However, an alternative definition of "ascension" is offered by author and spiritual teacher Leslie Temple Thurston, who uses the term to describe embodied spirituality—spirituality in which one is fully present in the body, with the recognition that body and spirit are one. Jungian analyst Marion Woodman has for decades been writing and teaching embodied spirituality. In a paper by Michael George Hofrath entitled "A Marion Woodman Perspective on the Embodied Psyche Experiential Integration," the author cites Woodman on the role of the body in the individuation or spiritual evolution process:

> *The forsaken body must be validated; given a voice, otherwise soma will resource a way to manifest this cry for acknowledgment in myriad ways, physical symptoms, psychic disturbance,*

nightmare imagery, or in dreams. Woodman (1985) states "Whether we like it or not, one of our tasks on this earth is to work with the opposites through different levels of consciousness until body, soul and spirit resonate together." Marie Louise Von Franz (as cited in Woodman, 1985) states "The only way the Self can manifest is through conflict to meet one's insoluble and eternal conflict is to meet God, which would be the end of the ego and all its blather." Body awareness, and the realization of the feminine consciousness, is a vital first step toward regaining one's lost, stolen, or given away soul skin, on the path for individuation and wholeness.[91]

Three decades ago, Buddhist psychologist John Welwood coined the term "spiritual bypassing." The term describes the efforts of some individuals to utilize spiritual practices to bypass or sidestep unresolved emotional issues or psychological wounding. According to Welwood, spiritual bypassing is an unhealthy response to our wounding. "Trying to move beyond our psychological and emotional issues by sidestepping them is dangerous. It sets up a debilitating split between the Buddha and the human within us. And it leads to a conceptual, one-sided kind of spirituality where one pole of life is elevated at the expense of its opposite: Absolute truth is favored over relative truth, the impersonal over the personal, emptiness over form, transcendence over embodiment, and detachment over feeling. One might, for example, try to practice nonattachment by dismissing one's need for love, but this only drives the need underground, so that it often becomes unconsciously acted out in covert and possibly harmful ways instead."[92]

In an article entitled "Spiritual Bypassing: Avoidance in Holy Drag," another Buddhist psychologist Robert Augustus Masters notes, "Spiritual bypassing is a very persistent shadow of spirituality, manifesting in many ways, often without being acknowledged as such. Aspects of spiritual bypassing include exaggerated detachment, emotional numbing and repression, overemphasis on the positive, anger-phobia, blind or overly tolerant compassion, weak or too porous boundaries, lopsided development (cognitive intelligence often being far ahead of emotional and moral intelligence), debilitating judgment about one's negativity or shadow side, devaluation of the personal relative to the spiritual, and delusions of having arrived at a higher level of being."[93]

As I persisted in my own Jungian depth therapy, I quickly came to understand the extent to which my reliance on New Age spirituality had served to mask my pain and obscure the deep childhood wounds I needed to attend to in order to experience the wholeness for which I longed. My obsession with positive thinking and attempting to manifest a pain-free life had fostered within me an ego-inflation that was rapidly *de*-flated as I became more familiar with the ugly, obnoxious aspects of my shadow.

Jung, who was profoundly influenced by his travels among indigenous cultures around the world, incorporated the wisdom of indigenous traditions into his work. When people become familiar with Jung or experience Jungian therapy, they often feel drawn to indigenous wisdom, which deeply resonates with the individuation process. As a result, the discovery of indigenous wisdom and its resonance with one's innate longing for intimacy with nature rapidly reveals

New Age spirituality as yet another manifestation of the Western corporate, capitalist agenda, imbedded in a ghastly estrangement from the Earth community.

The exclusively solar perspective could never have arisen in an indigenous culture. It is rooted in estrangement from the Earth and alienation from other human beings. Similar to the perspective of fundamentalist Christianity, there is little sense of community, but rather, "me and my spiritual journey." In a culture of industrialized consumerist narcissism, we can expect to see a variety of iterations of New Age spirituality with their disembodied relationships with the sacred.

The following table is an incomplete but essential summary of the disparate perspectives of the indigenous person and the student of New Age spirituality:

INDIGENOUS PERSPECTIVE VERSUS NEW AGE PERSPECTIVE

I come from the earth; to the earth I return	I come from Spirit. I was born in a body, but I am beyond the body.
The earth is my ultimate authority	The mind and my thoughts reign supreme.
Life is comprised of a variety of experiences, some painful, some neutral, some pleasant	I accept only positive thoughts and experiences.
I cannot survive without community	My journey is more important than community.
The earth abundantly meets my needs	My needs are met through positive thinking.
Conflict is good because it engages me with the community.	Conflict does not demonstrate the highest good which is harmony.
I need to be connected with land and place.	I can be anywhere because "there's not a spot where God is not."
Life involves a great deal of suffering and uncertainty interspersed with joy.	There is no need to suffer if I'm living in the light.
Human beings are complicated creatures with a wide range of emotions. I must accept those emotions in myself and others.	Only peace and love are real emotions. I choose to associate only with positive people.
All human beings have a dark side.	All human beings are light beings.

At this juncture in human history as we live with

the possibility of near-term human extinction, we must embrace indigenous wisdom, not because it can assist us in saving ourselves or saving the Earth, but because it reveals the magnificent depths and incomprehensible breadth of humanity. We frequently hear the statement that we are spiritual beings having a human experience. However, I prefer to reverse the statement, emphasizing that if we are on a spiritual path, we are human beings having a spiritual experience. It is in the depths of our humanity that we discover our more-than-human essence.

The global crisis compels us to step decisively into spiritual elderhood, which has little to do with age and everything to do with the cultivation of wisdom. The first advance toward spiritual elderhood is the mature decision to open to the reality of the shadow and become a willing student of its revelations, both personally within one's own psyche and collectively in the macrocosm.

Industrial civilization has hijacked our humanity and offers us myriad substitutes for it by seducing us into a consumeristic, narcissistic, entitled lifestyle, while offering philosophies that obscure this ghastly looting of the soul. Seething with an underbelly of brutal fundamentalism, New Age spirituality offers us dissociative denial, ensuring that we will never become conscious of the full range of our humanity nor the global crises that threaten to extinguish it permanently. Its finely-tuned mechanisms of spiritual bypassing guarantee that we will neither feel the pain of our own wounding or experience the shattering heartbreak of billions of innocent beings reeling toward extinction.

As my friend Andrew Harvey incessantly emphasizes, we must commit to engaging in some manner with indigenous wisdom. We can begin this adventure via the following three practices:

1) Developing an entirely different relationship with animals. We must engage not only with our pets, but open to the presence of animals in the rawness of nature;

2) Spending quality time in nature, not camping or hiking, or doing anything except being present— sitting quietly, contemplating, allowing all of our senses to engage with leaves, grass, trees, soil, insects, birds, streams, and the wildness that reminds us that we are nothing if not animal beings. Above all, in doing all of this, we must continually say, "Thank you."

3) Making a commitment to become a sacred activist in some capacity who allows radical heartbreak to guide us to whatever our mission is to be at this pivotal moment in the history of our planet. Whether or not that mission "succeeds" is not up to us. Our responsibility is to commit wholeheartedly regardless of the outcome.

As we engage with nature, we must know that we can never be separate from it. Everything in nature registers our presence when we humbly enter into communion with it. Every blade of grass, every leaf, every flower is changed because even as we enter nature, nature is looking back at us.

The *prize* of New Age spirituality is an ostensibly pain- free life. The *price* is disembodiment and a loss of communion with other beings in the suffering that is inherent in their existence and ours.

In Jungian circles, a story about Carl Jung is often told regarding his perspective on the "positive" and the "negative." For example, on one occasion, it is said that a client began a session relating that he had just lost his job and did not know how he was going to support his family. After listening to the client's tale of woe, Jung took out a bottle of champagne from his desk drawer, opened it, and said, "We must celebrate this occasion because this dark path, if you remain committed to it, will lead you to consciousness." On a very different occasion, a client began his session with Jung by elatedly sharing what he considered to be good news—getting a promotion, which would mean a larger income and a greater status in the company for which he was working. Upon hearing this, Jung shuddered and said, "This sounds like an inflation of the ego, and we must be very careful, but if we work hard on this together, we'll get through it." "Positive"? "Negative"? For Jung, things were not always as they seemed.

Are we willing to settle for the comfort of ignoring or disowning the shadow, or are we willing to settle for nothing less than surrendering everything and anything in order to experience the *Dark Gold*?

— — — — — — — — — — — —

SUGGESTED PRACTICES: Whether or not we currently embrace the New Age perspective described in Chapter 10, we have all engaged in some form of denial at some time in our lives. Non-indigenous people are imbedded in cultures that constantly invite them to participate in variety of forms of denial. Modern civilizations are the products of centuries of separation— from other humans and the Earth community. As a result of feeling nested in nature, indigenous people understand that the full spectrum of human experience is identical to the full spectrum experience of ecosystems. In other words, life holds moments of sorrow, pain, fear, disappointment, loss, anger, and anguish, but humans also have the capacity to weave within these so-called negative experiences moments of joy, beauty, conviviality, and magic. The following practices may be useful in assisting the reader in integrating the sacred and the mundane, light and dark, joy and sorrow, the spiritual and the human dimensions of one's experience:

1) Read the referenced articles in Chapter 10 on spiritual bypassing by John Welwood and Robert Augustus Masters. What most intrigued you in their writings on the topic? Did you find yourself identifying personally with anything they said about spiritual bypassing, if not in current time, perhaps in your past?

2. As you ponder the disparities between the indigenous perspective and the New Age perspective as outlined in the chart in Chapter 10, what do you notice? Are there other differences you would like to add?

3. How do you define spiritual elderhood? What qualities are included in your definition? How are you consciously seeking to develop your own spiritual elderhood?

4. The term "dark night of the soul" is often heard in psychological and spiritual venues. What is your

understanding of the term? Have you experienced what you would define as a dark night of the soul? If so, describe your experience. Did your experience, distressing as it was, in any way facilitate your appreciation of beauty, joy, love, nature, or community?

5. When we find ourselves drawn to an emphasis on positive thinking or spiritual perspectives that focus on living only in the light, we may also notice that the body is not fully grounded. New Age spirituality tends to emphasize spiritual, ephemeral, and mental states while de-emphasizing being present in the body. Deep breathing exercises as offered by Thich Nhat Hanh and other mindfulness teachers are helpful. So are more physical practices such as yoga, Qigong, or Tai Chi, which assist us in em-bodying spiritual experiences, bringing them home to the body where they become part of our physiology as well as our intellect. What physical practices are you engaged in that assist you in embodying spiritual truth? If you are not engaged in an embodied practice, consider doing so, and allow yourself to be drawn with the heart rather than the intellect. Then begin recording your experiences with these practices using journaling or artistic expression.

CHAPTER 11

BROKEN OPEN

MIRROR, MIRROR IN THE STREET

The image of the beggar entails a reversal of our attitude in consciousness. We may believe that we give him something, that we may contribute to his welfare. But the essence of his being is that he holds something for us to receive. He may hold in his hand, and whisper through his mouth, a wisdom free from conventional ethics, transcending our conscious distinction of good and evil. Beyond the blushing face of shame, the beggar's hand is full of emptiness—he holds nothing in his hand.
—Erel Shalit, "The Archetypal Beggar"

What is madness but nobility of soul at odds with circumstance?
—Theodore Roethke, "In a Dark Time"

'Cause you're a sky, cause you're a sky full of stars
I'm gonna give you my heart
And I don't care, go on and tear me apart And I
don't care if you do

> *'Cause in a sky, cause in a sky full of stars I think*
> *I see you*
> *I think I see you light up the path Such a heavenly*
> *vie You're such a heavenly view*
> **—Coldplay, 2014,"A Sky Full of Stars"**

Throughout this book we have explored numerous aspects of the personal and collective shadows, along with a variety of practices that may lead to their transformation. While structured practices may be salutary and surprisingly efficient, we must open our hearts and minds to life experiences that offer unanticipated, often unwanted, opportunities for shadow healing.

In this chapter I wish to step out of the role of teacher and simply tell an intimate story of encountering personal and collective shadows that pummeled me with heartbreak, humility, and compassion, and effectively compelled me to work more arduously with the shadow than I may ever had the capacity to do in a formal therapy setting or by implementing specific practices. The story is not particular to any specific city or community but is a composite of many communities, and in fact, could have occurred in any community in the world.

Following many months of doing intense shadow-clearing work with Leslie Temple Thurston's Marriage of Spirit Material (as suggested in Chapter 2 and expanded in the Appendix of this book), a spirit of generosity that I had never experienced awakened in me. Suddenly, I found myself taking a more keen interest in the homeless people in my community than I ever had. Whereas I rarely gave money to homeless people, assuming that they would only use it to buy drugs and alcohol, I no longer censored my contributions but rather began viewing them as simply spreading the energy of generosity without qualifying how that energy might be used.

On a cold March morning on my way to the gym where I regularly exercise, I stopped for a red light at an intersection where at nearly all hours of the day, one or more corners might be occupied by a homeless person "flying" a sign asking for money. As I was waiting for the light to turn green, I saw on one corner a bearded man and his dog, attended by the stereotypical homeless person's cart. The man was not waving a sign or doing anything to attract attention. In fact, he was very still. My eyes and heart alternately bounced from him to the dog and back to him. I felt deeply compelled to give him a couple of dollars.

Perhaps two months later while sitting outside and sipping a dessert coffee with friends behind a store not far from the intersection, I noticed the same man and dog sitting a few feet away. This time, I felt compelled to walk over to him and ask him for his and his dog's names. I followed the urge and was informed that the dog's name was Betty, and his was Buck. I returned to socializing with my friends, but I kept inconspicuously glancing at Buck and Betty out of the corner of my eye. I remained seated alone after my friends left and casually looked into my wallet to see if I had a few dollars to give Buck. To my surprise, all I had was a twenty-dollar bill. Reason screamed loudly that a donation of that amount was too generous, but my heart insisted that I give what at the moment was the last dollar in my wallet. I followed my heart and wished Buck and Betty a nice day.

Another month passed, and on yet another morning at

the infamous intersection, as I stopped for a red light, I saw Buck and Betty sitting on a different corner. A voice inside screamed that I must pull into a convenience store on that corner and talk with Buck. I followed the urge and struck up a conversation with him. I gave him two dollars and asked, "Where do you sleep?" His reply: Wherever he could do so without getting arrested, and he named a couple of locations, adding that at the moment, he had no camping tickets. Again, my departure was graceful, but the ache in my heart was anything but. I proceeded to the gym where my cardiac workout on the stationery bicycle produced the sensation of my heart exploding. My physical heart was fine, but my emotional heart was shattering. I jumped off the bike, drove to the nearest grocery store and bought a small bag of dog food and a four-pack of instant soups. I then raced back to the intersection, only to discover that Buck and Betty had disappeared.

For two weeks I kept the dog food and soups in my car and found myself driving all over town looking for the pair. I was on a mission, but to no avail because they were nowhere to be found. Finally, on yet another morning headed for the gym and stopped at the intersection, I saw them on the corner and bolted out of my car to give Buck the contents of the bag I had been carrying around for two weeks. I then asked if I could buy him lunch. He accepted the invitation, and I began a journey with Buck and Betty that I could have never anticipated. Only later did I learn that Buck and Betty were often encumbered with dog food that people contributed and that instant soups were not a realistic offering since most of the time, Buck had access only to cold water.

For more than three decades, mental health treatment in the United States has basically consisted of providing therapy and medication for the insured, while consigning the uninsured mentally ill to the streets to fend for themselves—and if they could not, incarcerating them. In fact, many homeless people are mentally ill (though many are not). As I proceeded to connect with Buck, I had no clue what his mental state might be. As a former psychotherapist, it was obvious to me early on that he was not psychotic. Clearly, he was struggling with bipolar disorder, a series of traumatic brain injuries, and PTSD, which he openly admitted. But not only was Buck not crazy, he was amazingly articulate and well-read. For at least an hour, we had an intelligent conversation as he told me his life story, and I shared a bit of mine.

Betty was quite dusty, and on that very hot day, it seemed that she might appreciate a bath. I asked Buck if I could treat her to a bath at a local pet store. He enthusiastically agreed, and we arranged to meet later that afternoon for a "spa experience" for Betty. Before parting, however, it felt important for me to state my boundaries and intention by telling Buck that I was not "girlfriend material," and that I wasn't in any financial position to assume the role of "sugar mama." He made no comment, merely nodding.

That afternoon we spent another hour talking as we waited for the groomers to finish working on Betty. Before I left my house to meet Buck at the pet store, I grabbed and signed a copy of my 2013 book *Collapsing Consciously*. I was fairly certain that he would appreciate it. In addition to the book, I gave him my cell phone number; I sensed nothing about him that produced any hesitation in doing so. When we parted, I told him to call me in a week.

Exactly one week later, almost to the hour, Buck called me, and we met again for lunch. After paying for our meals, I carried them outside where we sat at a table in a remote corner street-side. With his huge beard, somewhat intimidating sunglasses, ragged clothing, and cart, plus Betty lying on the sidewalk beneath his chair, we drew a series of curious, piercing stares. I could feel the judgment of onlookers: "I can't believe that lady is actually having lunch with that bum," or "Maybe she's a nun doing charity work."

In subsequent weeks as I accompanied Buck to the library, to medical appointments, and to the grocery store, I watched the myriad reactions. As people incredulously viewed both of us walking together and momentarily lost their ability to speak, I frequently stated, "I'm with him, and we need to…" So often I reflected on what it might have been like for Jesus to walk among his Pharisaical peers accompanying Mary Magdalene or one of the local lepers.

As I spent many hours a week with Buck and Betty learning about the social services bureaucracy, the daily realties of homelessness, and the physical dangers homeless people encounter regularly, my heart was broken open, and I could not stifle my generosity. I do not mean that I lost my boundaries, my sense of limits or personal needs, nor do I mean that I became a "bleeding heart" rescuer. Rather, I realized that I had entered into a relationship that had been designed by something greater than my human ego for the purpose of not only assisting Buck and Betty, but also educating me on myriad levels.

I had written volumes about the collapse of industrial

growth civilization, but the fact was, it was now in my face. Buck was living as many millions of people may be forced to live as the American empire crumbles and its economic accoutrements vanish. Thus, it was no surprise when his first response after finishing *Collapsing Consciously* was, "Finally, someone has written a book from my perspective!"

What makes homelessness so intolerable for so many non-homeless people to confront is the reality that some part of us really does know that there is no separation, and that the homeless person mirrors us in a manner that feels insufferable. We know in our bones that it could happen to us as surely as it has happened to them. When we see a homeless person, we are, in a sense, viewing ourselves— an experience that for the majority of middle class human beings in our culture is abjectly terrifying.

What do the homeless hold for us that we find intolerable to embrace? Quite frankly, they hold the shadow of our comfortable, industrially-civilized existence. When I say "comfortable," I do not mean that every person reading these words is rolling in riches. But anyone who is not homeless is more comfortable in terms of having their physical needs met than someone who has no other option than to sleep in the street or a homeless shelter.

The homeless hold up in our faces a larger-than-life portrait of what any one of us might be if our circumstances vary only slightly. For decades we've become accustomed to the expression "one paycheck away from homelessness"—five words that used to strike terror into our hearts but to which most of us have now become numb. Yet since the economic crash of 2008, the massive loss of full-time employment, the downsizing or disappearance of a variety of industries, the evaporation of billions of dollars in retirement savings, the loss of health insurance by unprecedented numbers of our population—in short, the burgeoning collapse of industrial civilization—the horror of homelessness is alive and well in our psyches, whether or not we are consciously aware of it. Homelessness increasingly becomes a real possibility for the middle and working classes, and our twisted logic tells us that if we blame the homeless, if we label them "sick," "crazy," or "lazy," somehow, it won't happen to us.

What do we see when we look at a homeless man or woman? We see a person who looks far older than they actually are. We see worn, rugged, and grungy faces. We see people without teeth, women without makeup or hair coloring. If we come close enough, we smell a variety of body odors and sometimes the stench of alcohol. We see and hear and smell and feel desperation, terror, depression, despair, rage, insanity, and a human being who has been reduced to a state that may resemble that of an animal in the wild. We see lives flattened, ripped apart, eviscerated, battered, broken, brutalized, assaulted, betrayed, and rejected more times than the mind inhabiting those bodies can even remember.

If we don't look at those faces, if we don't get too close, if we succeed in keeping them out of sight, we will have seduced ourselves into the delusion that homelessness will never happen to us. We may hand dollar bills out the car window. We may give to charitable organizations that serve the homeless, telling ourselves that it isn't our problem because it can't be solved and there are too many of them and our lives must go on.

Resentment may brew in our bones as we sit with being over 50 and without a job, because we got hosed in the crash of 2008 or we lost our retirement savings or we don't have health insurance anymore. We may think to ourselves about the homeless, "Yeah, you have it bad, but what about me? I'm an educated, law-abiding professional who had everything, and now I've lost it, and I'm going to make damn sure I never end up like you, so get out of my sight so I don't have to be reminded of what could happen to me." Or perhaps the twenty-something college graduate with a master's degree, who knows she will be paying off student loans until she is 80, can't find anything but part-time waitressing, has no health insurance, and will never be able to own a house thinks, "Man, don't talk to me about homelessness. I have two degrees, and every day I'm dancing on the edge of living in the street. Am I really much better off than they are?"

Buck often remarked that from his perspective I am actually a homeless person in disguise—a person who holds values similar to the homeless but outwardly appears to have embraced the values of civilization. He frequently teased me about getting rid of "the look" of civilization and dressing like who I really am inside. Even as I recounted to him my many years of donning hippie attire during the sixties, I could sense that he inwardly wanted me to abandon my lifestyle and join him in the homeless subculture of the streets. My response was simply to reiterate one of my core values, namely, that outward appearance matters much less to me than qualities of heart and character. Sometimes I challenged him by emphasizing that this value works both ways. I had befriended him because his inward qualities mattered to me much more than his external appearance. Only once in the beginning of our friendship did I naïvely suggest that he tidy up his appearance, and as our friendship deepened, I quickly realized the absurdity of my request. Thus, I reminded him that I had stopped expecting him to alter his external persona, and I wanted him to do the same with me because had we judged each other solely on outward appearance, we would have never formed the friendship we have today.

That was part of the magic and mystery of our connection. We looked and lived so differently, yet our hearts and minds joined across a vast chasm of socio-economic and cultural differences. I felt remarkable respect for Buck's resilience and adaptability, and at the same time, every part of me ached for his suffering. I feel gratitude for my capacity to be broken open and to feel the agony in my heart that results from the suffering Buck endures that I cannot take away.

I can be Buck's friend, and I can help him in some tangible ways, but perhaps the most important gift I can give him and all homeless people is the willingness to bear witness to his current experience. I can listen, I can care, I can be present—but most essentially, I can be willing to see what few people are willing to see, and I can allow myself to feel all that my seeing evokes in me.

Yet all was not congenial with every encounter I had with Buck. I soon realized that Buck had been dropped into my life to illumine and assist my confrontation with my personal and collective shadows. He had also shown up to perform what St. Teresa of Avila called "stretching the heart." Yes, my heart and been broken open, but often Buck spoke his truth to me in abrasive ways that pushed every button in my psyche. Like Buck, I too had grown up in an abusive home. Physical and psychological abuse were part of my daily childhood experience, as they were part of Buck's. One of the most sensitive wounds in my soul had resulted from being made an only-child scapegoat by parents who incessantly projected their personal shadows on me. The challenge for me was to hold unconditional love for Buck even as I was being mis- perceived, and from my perspective, often mis-treated.

I soon began thinking of Buck as my personal "bipolar bear." On some days, every encounter with Buck was a test —a test of how I could stand in love and yet notice how I felt when the arrows of false accusation flew at me. I wondered: Am I truly being abused? Does he really intend to hurt me? He's totally distorting what I'm saying or doing. This feels exactly like being a child in my mother's kitchen as I'm lectured for all the ways I'm wrong, inadequate, and worthless, followed by a slap or a beating with a belt just to make sure I "understood." Often my encounters with Buck were little more than the defensive posturing of two abused children attempting to spare themselves from more battering and verbal assaults.

On two occasions I lost my temper with Buck, and I recall these with shame and remorse as hot and molten as my rage. My heart was broken on those occasions because I had hurt him deeply and allowed myself to be provoked into reaction—reaction that caused me to become the face of his abusive mother who constantly raged at him and physically abused him almost daily. Clearly, he expected every woman to eventually become his violent mother, and now Buck had encountered my anger, which could only bounce him like a rubber ball back to his childhood.

As a result, I needed to make an agreement with him about how I would respond in the future when we found ourselves in conflict. Buck incessantly tested me and attempted to push me away. While I refused to exit his life, I needed to set limits on his provocation. Thus, I agreed that I would not lash out at him but simply let him know that I could not continue the conversation at the moment and needed to take space.

On numerous occasions I sat with him as he made cantankerous comments about me, or else criticized me for something I said or did which he had interpreted as insensitive, naïve, or intrusive. Occasionally, he could not tolerate my saying anything, and I found myself just sitting with him and listening to a quiet rant. In those moments, I felt my heart being stretched to the breaking point. The abused child in me felt as if I was being battered all over again, yet the adult woman understood that I was not. While none of this was pleasant or desirable, I was not a child dependent on the caretaking of my parents. At the age of sixty-something, I was far more resourced than a defenseless third-grader. I had the choice to sit with Buck and continue listening, or else take space and walk away. Sometimes I parted cordially and took space. At other times I chose to sit and listen to the criticism, feeling the arrows of hostility, but a part of me that I call my inner witness was marveling at how my personal shadow was being seen for what it was. Like a student needing to sit with a master teacher and learn grueling arithmetic sums, my shadow needed to sit with Buck and be illumined. On most of these occasions, I was astounded at how astute his perceptions were and how necessarily humbling the interaction was. In those torturous moments, I was consciously, actively, and painfully reclaiming my shadow projections, and as a result, my shadow was undergoing an excruciating but profound healing process.

The human ego is a necessary aspect of the psyche, as it allows us to function logistically in the world. Yet Carl Jung distinguished between the ego and the Self. From Jung's perspective, the Self is the sacred within the psyche. Jung had learned from the great wisdom traditions throughout history that the purpose of our human existence is the diminishment and transformation of the ego and the expansion of the Self. In Psychology and Religion, Jung wrote:

> *The Self grants new perspectives. When we can look at the ego from the viewpoint of the Self, we gain an objective understanding of the nature of the ego—its claim to be our identity, its sense of distinction and preeminence over the psyche's other functions, its preferences and tastes, its quests for personal growth and mastery, and its self-centered perspective (which is not a bad thing but rather a vital standpoint for our focus and protection). When we meet the Self, we realize that we have previously assigned some of the Self's functions to the ego simply because we did not know the Self, and the ego seemed to be the only part of us which could fill these roles.*
>
> *Now we can transfer some the ego's functions to that Self; for example, instead of allowing the ego to devise our goals, we accept the Self's goals, which are aligned toward the actualization of its*

> *life-purpose; the ego, without the wise, balancing*
> *influence of the Self, tends to select goals that are*
> *no more than ego-symbols, such as an audacious*
> *home.*[94]

To reiterate, a critical piece of the scapegoating I experienced as a child was being incessantly and unjustly accused of things I did not do. Not only did this experience shape my intolerance for injustice in all its forms, but it also created a deep wound in the ego regarding being seen for who I truly am. Thus, I became desperate to show the world who I really was, and therefore became hyper-vigilant about being falsely accused. As a result, when Buck attempted to "Other" me by calling me a yuppie or projected characteristics onto me that I felt were not warranted, I became defensive. In fact, Buck was fond of telling me how defensive I was, even as he needled and provoked me to defend myself. Consequently, my ego took a beating in my interactions with him, and eventually, it became unambiguously clear to me that this was exactly the point of my relationship with him. I needed to move to a place within myself where his opinion of me no longer mattered—where the divine within me loved him and myself so much that I could stand in the fire of his projections and not react. This is not to say that I was numb or that I ever moved beyond feeling hurt by them, but with each successive projection, I became more adept at holding alongside the sting, my love for Buck and for myself. For me, this constituted the ultimate expansion of my heart.

Often Buck thanked me for the myriad ways I had helped him and Betty. In fact, he once told me that had it not been for me, he and Betty might have been permanently jailed or simply not have survived a brutally cold winter.

Each time he expressed his deep gratitude, I reminded him of what he had done for me. I don't know that he will ever comprehend what that means, nor will he ever be able to fully grasp the dynamics of shadow projections and what it means to reclaim them. What I do know is that Buck has been one of the wisest teachers I've ever encountered.

But dancing emotionally with Buck in challenging conversations was not the only humbling experience to which I willingly subjected myself. After watching him "fly the sign," as homeless people refer to it, at the infamous intersection, sitting for long hours begging for money, I asked if I could join him. I recalled the words of Buddhist teacher and homeless advocate Bernie Glassman, who says, "When we bear witness, when we become the situation—homelessness, poverty, illness, violence, death—the right action arises by itself. We don't have to worry about what to do. We don't have to figure out solutions ahead of time. Peacemaking is the functioning of bearing witness. Once we listen with our entire body and mind, loving action arises."[95] I wanted to experience sitting in the street begging for money and feel what it was like, not only as an expression of empathy for my friend, but as a necessary spiritual practice.

So on an exquisitely beautiful, chilly autumn morning, I met Buck and Betty at the infamous intersection, and he instructed me to claim the corner where he usually sat when he worked the intersection, while he moved to the opposite side of the street and settled in with Betty and his cart. I was wearing the oldest, most worn-out clothes I had, and I was also wearing a floppy cotton hat for protection from the sun—or so I told myself. In fact, I knew very well that the hat and my sunglasses were protection from far more than the elements. They protected me from being recognized by friends who did not know of my connection with Buck, or from being fully exposed to complete strangers. First contradiction: I claimed that I wanted homeless people to be seen, but I didn't want to be seen, because my persona would be blown to smithereens. By definition, sitting there flying a sign invariably drew projections of being mentally ill, an addict, or both—a particularly challenging reality for a former psychotherapist. Pretending to be homeless and desperately poor meant not being seen at all for who I really am, but being perceived as someone else. And I had volunteered for this assignment. Another full body-blow to the ego

I could have made endless excuses to Buck and to myself for not going into the street and flying the sign, and the temptation to do so was at times nearly irresistible. Yet I knew that if I did not fly the sign and feel what homeless people feel, nothing I said in any of my books or workshops or public presentations would mean anything. This was where the rubber needed to meet the road. In *sitting* in the street pretending to be homeless, I was also *standing* with the mentally ill and with addicts, alcoholics, and all people marginalized by this culture. As a lesbian, I had lived on the margins all of my life, so I was not only familiar with the territory but preferred it. Now, however, I was traversing margins that felt profoundly life-threatening, and as I had essentially written in all of my books addressing the collapse of industrial civilization, I was practicing what I preached: *Become very familiar with what it might be like to lose everything, including your life.*

As I had known it would be, this was one of the most

humbling experiences of my life. I had voluntarily signed up to be seen as someone I'm not, and consented to open myself to a plethora of projections—a veritable extravaganza of being falsely accused. For me, it was worse than being naked, because being naked means being seen for exactly who one is. In this situation, I was not being seen at all, but willingly inviting the invariable projections, distortions, and fantasies that most individuals in this culture direct toward the homeless. I had agreed to become a scapegoat for as long as I maintained the persona of a panhandling homeless person, and since I had played the scapegoat role in my family of origin, I was also allowing myself to feel the agonizing emotions of that period of my life. As I sat in the street begging, the Audis, BMWs, and Escalades passed by incessantly. Almost no one looked, let alone saw me. As a result, the personal and collective shadows congealed in this ego-shattering experiment.

When we are confronted with painful dilemmas, we frequently have options about how we will respond to them. One option, if we have sufficient emotional resilience, is to fully embrace the challenge and creatively move with it, rather than resisting. After an hour of being ignored, I took off my hat, and magic happened. Let them see my silver hair and my sign that says "Anything Helps," I thought, and let's play the "Grandma" persona for all it's worth. Soon donations were popping, and I reluctantly embraced my role. On the one hand, it felt clever and creative, but another part of me was terrified. How many times had I sat with women my age who, like me, were skeptical of how long the corporate capitalist system could endure? Had we not joked cynically about the cost of war sucking the Social Security system and all other safety nets dry? Had we not mouthed snarky fantasies about having to live in a refrigerator box on the street in our old age? Whether they admit it or not, the bedrock fear of every aging middle class woman is that someday, she will be forced to become a bag lady and eat cat food—a predicament driven home to us in 1985 by Lucille Ball's stunning performance in the TV film series "Stone Pillow."[96]

Nevertheless, I danced on the edge of my fear and embarrassment and plunged with gusto into my "homeless, silver-haired bag lady" persona. I quickly realized that a particular "role" was putting me on a "roll." But what if it were all true? What if I had no income, no friends, no home? What if I were in poor health and dying of some horrible disease…and who says I won't? Part of me felt like a con artist, and I had to remind myself that I was "fundraising" for Buck. Yet another part of me knew that in terms of the experience and what it was teaching me, I wasn't sitting there pretending to be homeless for anyone other than me. I felt more arrows of projection as I imagined the stories people were making up in their minds about the silver-haired bag lady: *Where are her kids? Why aren't they taking care of her? What kind of stupid choices did she make to put herself in this position?*

I continued to sit at the intersection for another half hour, the warm sun blazing at my back as I gazed far into the distance to see what cars were heading my way. Once again, I found myself imagining the desperation of the homeless men or women who sit at that intersection seven days a week because they will not eat unless they beg—and begging is no guarantee that they will eat. Suddenly, a police cruiser pulled up to the intersection and stopped. I knew the officer was waiting for the light to change, but sitting in the street pretending to be homeless when a police cruiser is less than ten feet away does not transport one to gardens of serenity. Even as I knew that flying the sign at this intersection was largely ignored by the police, and that homeless people were not harassed here, I also knew that in some cities, homeless people are not allowed to beg in any intersection, and that a corner that was legal one day might not be the next.

The arrival of the police cruiser set me thinking about what I *would* say if I were ticketed by an officer for panhandling. Would I say, "Gee officer, I'm just playing a game. Actually, I'm a well-educated author who is doing a social experiment and picking up some chump change for my homeless friend." Or would I quietly accept my fine, pay it, and take my "role" to the limit, not pretending to be other than a homeless panhandler?

I gave the $19 and one candy bar that I received in two hours to Buck and told him about my "Grandma" persona. He remarked, "Looks like Grandma kicked some serious ass." We high-fived, and I later took him to lunch, as was our Saturday ritual. When we met up outside the restaurant, Buck removed his sunglasses and hat, looked me squarely in the eye, and said, "So what did you learn?"

I recounted my insights in detail, but what I failed to mention was that despite all of the emotions that passed through my body—the fear, embarrassment, despair, anger, and that oceanic deluge of humility that engulfed me, I experienced a profound sense of serenity and stillness at my core. I felt what may have been the most palpable feeling of "rightness" I had ever experienced. Externally, I was surrounded by the roar of traffic, the attendant exhaust fumes, and hundreds of people who for the most part ignored me; internally, a potpourri of emotions permeated my body. Yet this was exactly where I was supposed to be, and nowhere else would have been appropriate—because on that fall morning, I met the Buddha in the unlikeliest of places.

Will I continue to engage in this spiritual practice? I do not know with certainty, but I imagine I will—as well as in other places where the Buddha is waiting to find me. As the ancient Celtic story of "The King and the Beggar's Gift" so succinctly articulates:

> *There is an old story of a young king whose subjects were delighted when he inherited and brought many gifts. After the coronation, the new king was at supper in the palace, when there was a knock on the door. A servant answered and discovered an old, shabbily dressed man who was asking to see the king. The servant did his best to dissuade the old man, but to no avail.*

> *When the king came out to meet the old man, he praised the king for his many virtues, and gave him a melon as a gift. The king hated melons, but being a kind man took the fruit and thanked the old man. The old man went away happy, and the servant threw the melon out into an unused courtyard.*

> *The next week at the same time, there was again a knock on the door. The king was again summoned, and there was the old man with his*

praise and his melon. Throughout the summer it happened every week. The king was too kind to confront the old beggar or belittle his generosity, and each time accepted the gift and threw it out.

Then one evening just as the old beggar was about to hand the melon to the king, a monkey jumped down from a portico and knocked the melon from the old man's hand. The melon shattered in pieces, and when the king looked, he saw a shower of diamonds flying from the heart of the melon. Eagerly he checked the courtyard, and there all the melons had melted around a hillock of jewels.

In no way do I believe that because I flew the sign with Buck on two occasions that I am now qualified to be an expert on homelessness. I have never spent a night in the street, nor have I ever wondered if I could eat on a particular day. Eventually, I came to understand that when Buck called someone a "yuppie," he was not defining them according to their socio-economic status; rather, from his perspective as a homeless person, anyone who wasn't homeless was a "yuppie" by comparison.

I am grateful for the experience of flying the sign with Buck, because it put me solidly in his shoes and in the shoes of all homeless people. As with the king in the story above, the "jewels" that have fallen into my life as a result of my relationship with Buck have been incalculable.

When confronted by the sheer vulnerability and neediness of the homeless person, the non-homeless person is often frozen by one overriding conundrum: The person begging, we believe, is always an addict or an alcoholic, so that as much as we would like to be generous, another part of us wonders how the money will be used. I saw it in the faces of the people in their cars at the intersection who refused to look at me as I sat begging in the street. I felt it in my own body when I first began giving money to homeless people. I recall the voice in my head that said, "Yes, I know this is a way to express generosity in the world, but I worked hard for this money, and I don't want some homeless person using it to buy drugs or alcohol." For this reason, many people prefer to give food to the homeless person, or if the homeless person has a dog, provide food for the animal.

As I reflect on my reluctance to give money to the homeless earlier in my life, I don't recall ever questioning what a food server, a hair stylist, or a taxi driver would do with my tips. Were these individuals not equally capable of using my tips to buy drugs or alcohol? When I pay my federal income taxes, I know exactly where my money is going: to build weapons of mass destruction and finance endless war. When I pay my energy bill, I know where that money is going also: to frack more natural gas, devastate the environment, and acquire huge profits for the fossil fuel industry.

The lesson I needed to learn was that once I release the money—to whomever for whatever reason—it is no longer my money. In fact, I have come to understand that it was never "my" money in the first place. Moreover, if I expect a homeless person or any other person to use my gift in a particular way, I am claiming the money as mine, not releasing it, and thereby expecting something in return—a perspective that defies the authentic meaning of "gift."

Never before had this been as clear as when I sat in the intersection pretending to be homeless.

I am grateful to Leslie Temple Thurston for her incisive teachings on the concept of money as flow rather than a static object that we *get, possess, hoard, save, invest, or give away with expectation*. Money is energy—an energy intimately connected with the energy of love.[97]

THE SHADOW ARCHETYPE OF THE HOMELESS WANDERER

For all of the reasons stated above, it is very difficult for non-homeless people to bear witness to the homeless. Additionally, our perception of homelessness is influenced by archetypes such as the Beggar, Wanderer, Bag Lady, Little Match Girl, Cripple, and more. The human psyche contains all archetypes, but some are constellated throughout our lives, while others remain disengaged depending on our life experiences. In the most affluent society in human history, we can be certain that the Beggar archetype inhabits the shadow of nearly all individuals. As noted above, the shadow is simply all that we are not aware of in the psyche, particularly those parts of the human experience that we say are "not me." Thus, even in times of remarkable prosperity, the Beggar is alive and well in the shadow. Myriad situations trigger the fear of the Beggar within—situations such as home foreclosure, unemployment, loss of health insurance, divorce, bankruptcy, debt, money owed to the IRS, and more.

Yet the Beggar may reveal itself not only in issues related to money, but when we become desperate for love and attention, or when we manipulate to get what we want. When we beg for attention, love, power, or material objects, we act out the Beggar. People working for non- profit agencies or political groups who are engaged in fundraising are also living the Beggar archetype.

A particularly toxic distortion in this culture has been the myth of the American Dream, which we explored in Chapter 6. Although the American Dream has now been revealed as delusional for many individuals who were victimized by the financial collapse of 2007-2009, for centuries, Americans have embraced the notion of the self-made individual who works hard, plays by the rules, and pulls themselves up by their own bootstraps. Although the myth is teetering on the edge of demise for many and completely disowned by others, the more affluent continue to cherish the chimera. Nevertheless, the Beggar is alive and well in their psyches, because it is the shadow side of their prosperity. For this reason, to actually give money to a homeless person or directly interact with them in some way is anathema. To look a homeless person in the eye, shake their hand, or hug them is deplorable to such individuals, for whom writing a check to the local homeless shelter or another charitable organization serving the homeless is infinitely preferable—if that individual is willing to gift the homeless at all. The Beggar archetype feels life- threatening for some, and they will do whatever it takes to keep it at bay.

As with any archetype, if we become of aware of its presence and purpose in the psyche, we can develop a working relationship with it and learn what it wishes to teach us. Some have embraced the Beggar archetype in a positive fashion: Mother Theresa, for example, or the

Buddha himself, who voluntarily became homeless in order to complete his spiritual journey.

I do not wish to imply that everyone must relate to homeless people in the same manner I have. Not everyone feels drawn to dance with the Beggar as I am doing. Rather, I invite you, dear reader, to consider that as in the story of "The King And the Beggar's Gift" above, you open to the Beggar archetype and embrace the gifts it holds. Resolve to look beyond whether or not you "like" the gifts, and claim the diamonds in disguise. A host of diamonds awaits your discovery. One diamond may be the heart-expanding joy of giving to someone who desperately needs and appreciates what you offer. Yet other diamonds may hold less joy and require more tedious, ego-battering inner work regarding what the relationship with the external "Beggar" evokes in your own psyche.

HOMELESSNESS: HALTING THE HERO ARCHETYPE

Luke Skywalker, Moses, William Wallace, Wonder Woman, Joan of Arc—all are heroes or heroines that Western culture reveres for their bravery and courage. In more recent times, our heroes have originated in the corporate world, or as a result of financial triumph. A particularly significant American myth evolved from the nineteenth-century tale of Horatio Alger—a man of humble origins who took a menial job in a factory and through honesty and hard work, garnered the attention of the boss, eventually marrying his daughter. Subsequently, Alger wrote a series of "rags to riches" novels that perpetuated the myth of the self-made man. In addition, the nineteenth century with its outrageous oppression of workers and the poor spawned a number of similar stories around the theme of the self-made man: Work hard, play by the rules, pay your bills, do not question authority, and success is guaranteed. Thus, the American Dream was born.

Unlike the modern hero who is venerated for conquering external territory, The Hero archetype is prevalent in ancient Greek mythology, and the mission of the Hero was also conquest, but not necessarily conquest of external territory, rather discipline and the submission of personal ambition in service to the gods. Frequently, the Hero was tempted with hubris—that is, the belief that he could become wiser and more powerful than the gods—and his challenge was to exemplify for the community how one overcomes hubris. Although the hero was always flawed, he was usually valiant, inspiring, and wise.

However, when a culture becomes obsessed with the Hero archetype, it fixates on progress, deploring regress or anything less than unequivocal advancement. As we can see in the tycoon's triumph as he rises to the top of the American Dream, the deeper, sacred meaning of the Hero is lost, and his significance is trivialized and made profane.

HOMELESSNESS = DEATH

Not only is Western civilization preoccupied with ego-based heroism, it is profoundly death-phobic. With the exception of the Irish and their passionate death wakes, Western culture frantically avoids the topic of death, failing to grasp that death is a part of life. In more recent years, pioneers in death and dying research such as Elisabeth Kubler-Ross and Stephen Levine have persisted in keeping the topic alive in our consciousness. Moreover, within the past decade, a number of Death Cafés have proliferated in the United States, offering opportunities for people to meet in safe, supportive environments to discuss an otherwise-forbidden subject. (A death café "is a group discussion of death with no agenda, objectives or themes. It is a discussion group rather than a grief support group or a counseling session.") http://deathcafe.com/what/

When we see a homeless person, we are essentially viewing a societal corpse who may be walking around alive and animated, but who represents death and loss— the death of dreams; the death of livelihood; the loss of home, family, place, and a sense of belonging. Heroes, we believe, do not experience significant losses, and they appear vitally alive at all times. In this culture, heroes ascend, reach pinnacles of success, and if they fall, then they were never authentically heroic. Conversely, often the persona of a homeless person points downward— drooping attire, slumped posture, and unmitigated downward mobility. Moreover, most of us are well aware of the physical perils of being homeless—being physically assaulted or murdered, or dying from exposure, lack of healthcare, or a terminal disease. The very acts of living in the street and begging for money not only emblazon the word "loss" in our consciousness, but reveal what being near "death's door" looks like.

The financial collapse of 2007-2009 engendered a massive transfer of wealth from the middle class and poor strata of American society to Wall Street. As a result, "success" was not redefined, but the number of people who could attain it was. Thus, vast numbers of college graduates in the twenty-first century enter a world in which they are carrying crushing student loan debt, and where employment is so difficult to acquire that many find themselves forced to move back home with parents so they can save some money or simply stay afloat while being underemployed. These new graduates might not be able to afford health insurance or a car, let alone ever purchase their own home. Conversely, the wealthiest tier of society has grown obscenely more prosperous, and the most dramatic divide in income since the Great Depression is currently a fact of twenty-first century life in industrial growth societies.

Nearly a decade has passed since the beginning of the financial crisis, and unemployment, diminished purchasing power, and the unattainability of the American Dream has only been exacerbated. Many middle class Americans still cherish the belief that "things will turn around eventually because they always do," but most middle class and working poor understand that the "good times" of the eighties and nineties will continue to fade into increasingly distant memory. The party is unequivocally over.

Throughout the post-World War II era, Americans wildly embraced the heroic mentality. And as New Age spirituality burgeoned in the eighties, the mantra on many lips was "Every day, in every way, everything is getting better and better." Before the financial crisis, if you didn't appear to be achieving the American dream, it was your fault—and to a large extent, it still is. In her hard-hitting book *Bright-Sided: How Positive Thinking Is Undermining America*, Barbara Ehrenreich writes that Americans have become intoxicated with optimism and positive thinking, attended by the notion that poverty is some sort of character defect:

> *But the economic meltdown should have undone, once and for all, the idea of poverty as a personal shortcoming or dysfunctional state of mind. The lines at unemployment offices and churches offering free food include strivers as well as slackers, habitual optimists as well as the chronically depressed. When and if the economy recovers we can never allow ourselves to forget how widespread our vulnerability is, how easy it is to spiral down toward destitution.*
>
> *In addition, positive thinking has made itself useful as an apology for the crueler aspects of the market economy. If optimism is the key to material success, and if you can achieve an optimistic outlook through the discipline of positive thinking, then there is no excuse for failure. The flip side of positivity is thus a harsh insistence on personal responsibility: if your business fails or your job is eliminated, it must because you didn't try hard enough, didn't believe firmly enough in the inevitability of your success. As the economy has brought more layoffs and financial turbulence to the middle class, the promoters of positive thinking have increasingly emphasized this negative judgment: to be disappointed, resentful, or downcast is to be a "victim" and a "whiner."*[98]

No wonder the homeless are not seen, or when they cannot be avoided, they are met with contempt. No wonder we make up stories about how and why they have lost everything, but somehow, it could never happen to us. They reflect back to us the shadow concealed by our own wellbeing, regardless of how abundant or spare our economic status may be.

So often, our poets bring us back to the heart where we must struggle with the issue of homelessness: How did it happen? What part did each of us play in it? Where is the Beggar archetype in us, and what gifts does the Beggar hold for us? Why is it important for us to embrace the death that homelessness represents? Whether or not we choose to personally interact with a homeless person, the larger issue is how we can most compassionately respond. In his 1963 song "There but for Fortune," Phil Ochs sings:

> *Show me an alley, show me a train*
> *Show me a hobo who sleeps out in the rain*
> *And I'll show you a young man with many*
> *reasons why There but for fortune, may go you*
> *or I.*

Unless you, dear reader, understand that you may well be the next Buck, your heart will not be broken open, and the Beggar's diamonds will not be yours. But if you are willing to dance on the edge of uncertainty with the myriad ways the shadow manifests in your life, you may not be able to contain the jewels that fall into your lap.

— — — — — — — — — — —

SUGGESTED EXERCISE: Sooner or later, the personal shadow emerges in every human relationship. Following are two helpful exercises:

1) Take time to reflect through journaling or artistic expression on how the shadow has shown up in a relationship. How has the shadow of the other person revealed itself? How has your own shadow appeared? What emotions resulted? What did you learn from these manifestations of the human shadow in this relationship?

2) The following questions comprise a series entitled "The Homeless: 39 Questions." Ponder these questions, being aware of what you feel as you do so. [The Homeless: 39 Questions: www. kindnessblog.com/2014/10/01/the- homeless-39 -questions-for-your-reflection/]

1. When you see a homeless person, do you look the other way and keep on walking?
2. Do you avoid making eye contact?
3. Is there a sudden selective deafness when you "hear," or don't "hear," their requests for help?
4. If you do ignore a homeless person's request for help, just how quickly does the incident evaporate from your mind?
5. Seconds? Minutes? Hours?
6. What is your honest opinion of these people who are teetering on the very edges of our society?
7. Do they you feel that, possibly, they deserve their predicament?
8. Could it be that they are lazy?

9. If so, should they simply get off their lazy rear- ends and look for a decent job?

10. Is it easy to get a job where you live?

11. Do you think it is any easier to get a job where you live if you're homeless?

12. Have you considered that there are homeless people who do have regular jobs?

13. Does your suspicion that some of these people might be pulling a con and actually making good money by pretending to be homeless and begging stop you from helping any of them?

14. Do you feel a sense of disgust or detest the way they smell, look, sound or behave?

15. Do you have any personal experience of homelessness?

16. Could you handle being homeless day after day and keep things together?

17. Would you smell better, behave better or beg less than a homeless person does if you did not have a home to go to for the next four weeks?

18. Are the homeless asking for money because, in the main, they want to buy drugs and/or alcohol?

19. If so, is that why you won't help them?

20. Can you see that if you were homeless you might also want to take something to numb your feelings about the situation?

21. Do you think the homeless are completely beyond our ability to help?

22. Is it that they should pull themselves up by their own bootstraps?

23. Would you prefer them to be "relocated" away from your line of sight so that they can also be put out of your mind?

24. What are your thoughts on the concept of homelessness being a crime?

25. Do you see homeless people and hear yourself muttering internal sound bites like, "There but for the grace of God go I"?

26. Are you worried that homeless people's craziness, anger, or diseases are contagious?

27. Were the homeless born homeless, addicted, or mentally ill?

28. How close are you right now to being homeless?

29. How many missed salary payments would it take?

30. How many family members or friends would let you stay at their house?

31. How long would they let you stay?

32. Are you sure about that?

33. What would a bad divorce, redundancy, or severe mental illness do to you?

34. Do you have a clear idea of just how far any one of us can fall and how quickly it can happen?

35. Are you immune from losing everything that you care about?

36. What is your response to these people who have less than you or nothing at all?

37. What is your response to a man or woman begging for food?

38. Do you help; smile; offer something, anything; buy them food; stay there for a moment and engage in a conversation?

39. Are you somehow better than the homeless, or just better off?

CHAPTER 12

REDEMPTION, TAKING BACK PROJECTIONS, TRANSFORMING THE SHADOW

> *The discovery of the unconscious is one of the most far-reaching discoveries of recent times. But the fact that recognition of its unconscious reality involves honest self-examination and reorganization of one's life causes many people to continue to behave as if nothing at all has happened. It takes a lot of courage to take the unconscious seriously and to tackle the problems it raises.*
>
> **—Marie LouiseVon Franz, The Realization of the Shadow**

> *If more people do not try to reflect and take back their projections and take the opposite within themselves, there will be a total destruction*
>
> **—Marie LouiseVon Franz,"Matter of Heart"**

The late Debbie Ford offers one of the most succinct and coherent explanations of the dynamic of projection in her book *The Dark Side of the Light Chasers*:

Projection is a fascinating phenomenon they failed to teach most of us about in school. It is an involuntary transfer of our own unconscious behavior onto others, so it appears to us that these qualities actually exist in the other people. When we have anxiety about our emotions or unacceptable parts of our personalities, we attribute these qualities—as a defense mechanism —to external objects and other people. When we have little tolerance for others, for example, we are likely to attribute the sense of our own inferiority to them. Of course, there's always a "hook" that invites our projection. Some imperfect quality in other people activates some aspect of ourselves that wants our attention. So whatever we don't own about ourselves we project onto other people.

We see only that which we are. I like to think of it in terms of energy. Imagine having a hundred different electrical outlets on your chest. Each outlet represents a different quality. The qualities we acknowledge and embrace have cover plates over them. They are safe: no electricity runs through them. But the qualities that are not okay with us, that we have not yet owned, do have a charge. So when others come along who act out one of these qualities they plug right into us. For example, if we deny or are uncomfortable with our anger, we will attract angry people into our lives. We will suppress our own angry feelings and judge people whom we see as angry. Since we lie to ourselves about our own internal feelings, the only way we can find them is to see them in others. Other people mirror back our hidden emotions and feelings, which allows us to recognize and reclaim them.

We instinctively draw back from our own negative projections. It's easier to examine what we are attracted to than what repels us. If I am offended by your arrogance it is because I'm not embracing my own arrogance. This is either arrogance that I am now demonstrating in my life and not seeing, or arrogance that I deny I am capable of demonstrating in the future. If I am offended by arrogance I need to look closely at all areas of my life and ask myself these questions: When have I been arrogant in the past? Am I being arrogant now? Could I be arrogant in the future? It would certainly be arrogant of me to answer no to these questions without really looking at myself, or without asking others if they have ever experienced my being arrogant. The act of judging someone else is arrogant, so obviously all of us have the capacity to be arrogant. If I embrace my own arrogance, I won't be upset by someone else's. I might notice it, but it won't affect me. My arrogance outlet will have a cover plate on it. It is only when you're lying to yourself or hating some aspect of yourself that you'll get an emotional charge from someone else's behavior.[99]

This incisive assessment by Ford, which pertains to the personal shadow, deserves further examination. She observes that when we transfer our projection onto someone else, it appears that they possess the quality that we project onto them. I hasten to add that the issue is not that the other person does not possess the quality we project. Rather, as

Ford notes, there is always a "hook" on which we can hang the projection. For example, one may protest that someone is "controlling," which may be a quality in oneself that has not been owned. The other person may or may not be controlling in a particular situation, yet the person projecting generalizes that the other is a "controlling person." In fact, the other may or may not be a controlling person, but something in her serves as a hook that invites the projection. She may take charge in a particular situation, or hold an assertive demeanor, or simply maintain healthy boundaries that serve to protect her or others in the situation. In different circumstances, she may not be controlling. But for the person projecting, the behavior of the other is perceived as controlling in general, because the person projecting has not owned their desire to control. The "electrical outlet" called "control" on the psyche of the projecting person has no cover; therefore, a "charge" is incited by the person onto whom they are projecting. The person projecting the quality of "controlling" can take the first step in alleviating the conflict by owning their own unconscious tendencies to control. While this may have no direct effect on the other who is perceived as controlling, the projecting person is thereby placing a "plate" over the electrical outlet of control in their own psyche, and doing so will invariably alter how they relate to the other. As a result, the relationship may become more harmonious.

However, it may be unimaginably agonizing to personally own the quality that one is projecting onto the other. How do we begin to admit and accept that some part of us is controlling, arrogant, jealous, self-absorbed, competitive, condescending, patronizing, or even vicious and violent? This is the anguish of doing shadow work because admission of these dreaded characteristics is almost always attended by toxic shame.

Toxic shame is not the same as appropriate guilt. Guilt is a sense of culpability and a recognition that one bears responsibility for something one has done or said that has been hurtful to another (and also perhaps to oneself).

Guilt never feels good, but one may respond to it by making amends to the injured party and making restitution if possible. When we experience guilt, we are humbled, and recognize, often with great pain, that we are fallible human beings. In one sense, guilt allows us to join with other humans in the common experience of imperfection.

Conversely, toxic shame engulfs us with a sense of worthlessness and self-hatred. In fact, rather than reinforcing our human fallibility, it catapults us into the territory of sub-human inferiority. We find ourselves submerged in self-loathing and a feeling of being irreparably despicable.

None of us delights in feeling guilty, but it is eminently preferable to the experience of toxic shame, which I believe abides in the personal shadow of most inhabitants of industrial civilization. Few human beings raised predominantly in indigenous cultures carry the toxic shame at their core that contemporary Western humans carry. Myriad cultural factors account for this discrepancy, but toxic shame is a byproduct of the subtle "Othering" that is inherent in the milieu of industrial civilization. Ultimately, it is a merciless "Othering" of oneself as a result of one's estrangement from the Earth and human communities.

As noted in Chapter 7, in regard to the potential extinction of the human species, I stated: "The fact that humans are destroying the planet—and that they know this—floods us with dread and makes the collective and personal shadows even more dark and deadly. The potential of near-term human extinction created by our species lingers like a dark cloud of radioactive fallout in the collective shadow which has a demonic life of its own, exacerbating the treachery of the personal shadow of each individual." If this is so, could it be that the collective shadow is marinated in toxic shame, and then, rather than being owned and worked with, this toxic shame is projected onto myriad "others" globally?

In a brilliant article entitled "Shadow Projection: The Fuel of War," Jungian therapist Paul Levy writes:

> *Shadow projection is itself the unmediated expression, revelation and playing out of the shadow. Shadow projection, the process in which we "demonize" our enemies, entrancing ourselves into believing that "they" are inhumane monsters who need to be destroyed, is the underlying psychological process which, when collectively mobilized, is the high-octane fuel which feeds the human activity of war.*[100]

When we shadow project, says Levy, we hypnotize ourselves into relating to our own shadow as if it is outside of ourselves. Jung talked about "…the overweening pretensions of the human shadow, which we so gladly project on our fellow man in order to visit our own sins upon him with apparent justification."[101]

In other words, could it be that in the throes of this unprecedented crisis of potential human extinction, the collective shadow has gone berserk with projection and with waging war, all because humans cannot bear to unflinchingly view the shadow and therefore feel compelled to project it?

Again, astutely and with scorching clarity, Levy asserts:

> *In the act of shadow projecting, we perpetrate violence (both psychic and/or physical) not only on ourselves, but on the "other" who is the recipient of our shadow projection. This act of external violence is nothing other than our inner process of doing violence to a part of ourselves changing channels and expressing itself in, as, and through the external world. In trying to destroy our projected shadow in the outer world, however, we act out, become possessed by and incarnate the very shadow we are trying to destroy....In shadow projecting, we become bewitched by our own reflected and disowned shadow, thinking it exists objectively, separate from ourselves. In trying to destroy our own shadow, we find ourselves in an endless conflict with no "exit strategy" that, moment to moment, we ourselves are unknowingly feeding, supporting and creating. Trying to destroy our own projected shadow is a genuine form of madness, as it is an insane battle that can never be won. It is like trying to extinguish a fire by pouring gasoline on it.*[102]

REDEMPTION

How then, in the midst of the horrors our species has created collectively and which reflect the personal shadows of billions of human beings, do we heal both the personal and collective shadows? And will doing so prevent the extinction of the human species and the revitalization of our planet?

In addition to the practices I have suggested throughout this book and that I will suggest at the end of this chapter, I offer a personal story of shadow healing that may serve you, dear reader, and others with whom you may choose to share it.

In this seventh decade of my life, I reflect with penetrating discernment on the personal shadow with which I have consciously struggled for more than 30 years. It was tragically enhanced by familial child wounding and many forms of abuse. Nevertheless, in recent years, I have become painfully aware that I must move beyond my own personal "woundology" and the traumatic upbringing I suffered into a more astringent maturity with respect to the shadow. The agonizing truth is that I have harmed many people in ways of which I am aware, as well as in other ways that escaped my notice as I obliviously careened through life with entitled self- absorption. Long overdue appropriate guilt has repeatedly broken my heart as I ponder the careless and cavalier antics of the shadow and its damage to those I loved most. While I resist using religious terminology, I have needed to embrace a certain "penance" for my behavior which cannot undo it, but which has served to fashion me into a more compassionate and merciful human being.

Art often resonates not only with our current and past experiences, but also experiences yet to come, painful as they may be, that the psyche knows will be necessary for our wholeness. Thus, as I watched the 1986 movie "The Mission,"

I witnessed in a particular scene entitled "Redemption" an image that mirrored the "penance" required for my own shadow healing.

For those who have not viewed "The Mission," starring Robert De Niro as Rodrigo and Jeremy Irons as the priest, here is the IMDb website's synopsis of the "Redemption" scene:

> *Mercenary and slaver Rodrigo Mendoza (Robert De Niro) makes his living kidnapping natives and selling them to nearby plantations, including the plantation of the Spanish Governor Cabeza. Mendoza subsequently finds his fiancée and his younger half-brother Felipe in bed together. He kills Felipe in a duel. Although he is acquitted of the killing by Cabeza, Mendoza spirals into depression. Father Gabriel visits and challenges Mendoza to undertake a suitable penance. Mendoza accompanies the Jesuits on their return journey, dragging a heavy bundle containing his armor and sword. After initially tense moments upon reaching the outskirts of the natives' territory, though they recognize him, the natives embrace a tearful Mendoza and cut away his heavy bundle.*[103]

Rodrigo is clearly a brutal, womanizing character who has profited handsomely from the slave trade. In this remote South American village, his most despicable characteristics become more egregious until a moment of clarity, resulting from depression, opens him to the penance offered by Father Gabriel. For me, words fail to capture the essence of Rodrigo's redemption, but I have never been able to view the scene without being shaken to my core, for it resonates so profoundly with my own "redemption." (I encourage the reader to view the scene at: www.youtube. com/watch?v=wzhhFRqjF_o)

Every individual is offered a "redemption" moment— or perhaps many in a lifetime. As with Rodrigo, such a moment may arrive with depression, trauma, betrayal, loss, or illness. The human ego cannot plan or orchestrate such a moment; it seems to arrive unexpectedly in a groundswell of grace.

Redemption moments do not guarantee immunity from any ills of the human condition. In "The Mission," Rodrigo is ultimately killed after breaking his vows with the military and committing to defend the mission with his life. But shadow healing is never about "happily ever after." It is about a willingness to experience heartbreak, humbling, remorse, grief, and radical heart-opening, and then making restitution where possible. Rodrigo died attempting to save the mission, and each of us in current time who commit to shadow healing must find and commit to our "mission."

And how do we find our "mission" if we do not already know it? As Andrew Harvey writes in The Hope: A Guide to Sacred Activism, "When you can locate your deepest heartbreak and face your deepest heartbreak, then you will be guided to your most profound mission. Your deepest mission is hidden in your deepest heartbreak."[104]

MAKING AMENDS

In Twelve-Step programs around the world, individuals in recovery are urged to practice the Steps daily. Several Steps involve making amends to individuals that one has harmed. Specifically, Step Eight requires making a list of all persons one has harmed and being willing to make amends to them all. In many cases, it is not possible to make amends in person because the person harmed may be deceased or unwilling to communicate with the person making amends. In such instances, the person making amends is encouraged to write a letter that will not be sent in which they "take a searching and fearless moral inventory" (Step Four) of the harm they have done and allow themselves to feel the pain the harm has caused the other and themselves.

What is extraordinary about the Twelve Step amends process is that it does not permit vague, blanket apologies of "I'm sorry" or "Forgive me for anything I've done to hurt you." The recovering individual is required to think and feel deeply about the ways they have harmed the other and the ways they have harmed themselves in the process.

In this respect, certain moments of shadow work may be excruciating. Look again at the pain on Rodrigo's face as he climbs the mountain carrying his heavy burden. Register the sobs that pour from his heart as the burden is cut loose from his body. In my own experience, the longer I live, the more gratitude I feel for my life, and at the same time, the more remorse I feel with respect to people I have harmed— and there are many. To some I have made amends and restitution. With regard to others, amends are not possible, and in a sense, this book has been, among other things, my attempt to embrace those with whom I cannot have direct contact for the purpose of practicing my own Step Eight. It is part of my "searching and fearless moral inventory"—a further extension of my "Restoration."

Jungian psychotherapist Jenna Lilla writes, "It takes time and patience to work with the shadow element in ourselves. Carl Jung's work is a testament to the power of doing such work, and of being honest with ourselves. It is through the process of pulling back our projections that our personality (and our true being) comes fully into the world. And from this place we can come into a deeper and truer relationship with the world around us."[105]

In this moment, humanity stands on the knife's edge of survival or extinction. The scientific probabilities regarding the future are bleak at best. The challenge before us is not so much about insuring the survival of our species (which may no longer be feasible), but rather, how will we meet whatever the future holds with love and service to the Earth community. However, our desire to champion and serve all living beings through love in action cannot be skillfully employed unless the personal and collective shadows are recognized and engaged.

In *Owning Your Shadow*, Jungian analyst Robert Johnson writes, "Any repair of our fractured world must start with individuals who have the insight and courage to own their shadow....The tendency to see one's shadow 'out there' in one's neighbor or in another race or culture is the most dangerous aspect of the modern psyche."[106] Nevertheless, a willingness to engage and work with the shadow is sacred work—or as Johnson notes, "To own one's own shadow is to reach a holy place—an inner center—not attainable in any other way."[107]

We commit to shadow work not only to reach a holy place, but to transform our relationships with all beings and all things, and that transformation is the dark gold that results from wrestling with the personal and collective shadows. If we are to transcend the illusion of separation from the Earth community and members of our own species—if we are to cease "Othering" and experience profound psycho-spiritual union with creation—the personal and collective shadows must be engaged and healed. While it is humanly impossible to heal every aspect of the shadow, and while the collective shadow is monumental, we can begin the journey of withdrawing our projections and thereby cease contributing our personal shadow material to the larger whole.

As author and social commentator Andrew Bard Schmookler puts simply in his book Out of Weakness: Healing the Wounds That Drive Us to War:

> *Evil in the human psyche comes from a failure to bring together, to reconcile, the pieces of our experience. When we embrace all that we are, even the evil, the evil in us is transformed. When the diverse living energies of the human system are harmonized, the present bloody face of the world will be transformed into an image of the face of God.*[108]

SUGGESTED PRACTICES: Many individuals assume that "redemption" is a religious concept, but in fact, it is not.

Derived from the Latin word *redemptio*, redemption is more of an economic term than a religious one. It implies buying back, releasing, ransoming; and more specifically, in terms of the human shadow, reclaiming. In order to experience psychological redemption, it is necessary to take back or reclaim the shadow's projections, as explained in Chapter 12 and throughout this book. Reclaiming projections is often a protracted process, but the following are a few tools that offer steps for beginning the journey:

1) View Roland Joffe's 1986 movie "The Mission" in its entirety. As you watch the "Redemption" of Rodrigo, what do you feel? Do you personally identify with him in any way? Have you ever experienced this kind of "psychological penance"? If so, what was the outcome?

2) Journaling: Projections can be both positive and negative. We have all experienced the projections of other people on us, and we have all engaged in projecting on other people. What negative projections have you carried for another person(s)? When have you projected a negative emotion or attitude onto another person? What positive projections have you carried for another person(s)? When have you projected a positive emotion or attitude onto another person(s)?

Note that both positive and negative projections may be harmful simply because they *are* projections. Authentically valuing the positive aspects of another person as well as being able to be present with their negative qualities is only possible as a result of taking back all of our projections on them.

3. All humans project, and we do so as a way of protecting and defending ourselves from negative feelings. At the root of all projection is an intense emotion that we are unconsciously or consciously trying to avoid. When you have projected onto another person, what feelings were you attempting to avoid?

4. It takes enormous courage to reclaim our projections and become accountable. This can only happen if we allow ourselves to feel the distressing feelings instead of projecting them. Have you ever experienced consciously wanting to project but stopping yourself from doing so? Journal about what that experience was like. What was the outcome?

5. Is there anyone to whom you feel you owe amends? What barriers seem to impede doing so? If you are unable to make amends to this person (whether they are living or dead) consider writing a letter you are not going to send, in which you verbalize in detail your part in the separation that has occurred. If the person is alive, consider making amends in person if possible. Notice the feelings you experience when considering taking this step. Remember that making amends is for your benefit as much as for the benefit of the other person.

Appendix

Victim/Tyrant/Rebel/ Savior Exercise

Much of Marriage of Spirit by Leslie Temple Thurston is devoted to specific tools for understanding and healing the shadow. In the following exercise, "The Square," you create a grid in order to examine the shadow and discover aspects of the shadow that may not be presently conscious. This technique is called "processing."

The grid is created by drawing a vertical line down the center of a page, and a horizontal line across the page about mid-way down. This results in four quadrants. At the top of the upper left quadrant, write "Desire to…" and at the top of the upper right quadrant, "Desire not to…". Then, at the top of the lower left quadrant, write "Fear of…" and at the top of the lower right quadrant, "Fear of not…".

You could begin to process the Victim/Tyrant/Rebel/ Savior dynamic using some of the examples below. However, it is important to compose your own list in each of the quadrants. If the suggested items in each quadrant below do not fit your process, feel free to eliminate them, and certainly feel free to add others.

*** I recommend spending at least one hour on each set of squares, allowing everything to come up that wants to come up and then writing it down. After completing the squares, it is very important to offer them up to spirit, one's higher self, the Earth, and the universe, and ask for a clear and definite shift in consciousness. Leave the squares and do something completely different. A few days later, go back to your sets of squares and notice if anything has shifted in you and also if there is more to add.

Desire To Be A Victim	Desire Not To Be A Victim
• I don't have to be responsible • People empathize with me • I may be taken care of • My victimhood highlights how bad the other person is • Some people try to help/ rescue me • I get to feel special/ superior • I get to feel righteous and persecuted for my beliefs or behavior • I get to feel old and familiar feelings of shame. Even though they are unpleasant, they're familiar • I can become dependent which is much easier	• I don't want to be irresponsible • I want people to care about me because they really care, not because I'm a victim • I hate the notion of being a Victim • I don't want to be dependent • I don't want to feel disempowered • I don't like feeling shame • I don't want to be rescued.

Fear Of Being A Victim	Fear Of Not Being A Victim
• Being a Victim feels helpless and terrifying like death • I don't like feeling powerless • I feel like a big screw-up • I feel vulnerable • I want to take care of myself • People don't respect Victims	• If I'm not a Victim then people will blame me and say it's my fault • If I'm not a Victim I may have to do a lot of things I don't know how to do or don't feel capable of doing • I won't get the help I need • I won't feel special; I'll feel average like everyone else • If I'm not a Victim then it lets the Tyrant off the hook

Desire To Be A Tyrant	Desire Not To Be A Tyrant
• It makes me feel superior • I feel powerful • I feel special • I get to vent my anger • I feel more alive • People won't mess with me • I set things right • People admire/respect me • I feel useful • I feel righteous	• I really don't want to offend people • I feel ashamed when I'm acting like a Tyrant • I really don't want people to fear me • I'd rather feel useful without being a Tyrant • I'd like to find another way of getting what I want

Fear Of Being A Tyrant	Fear Of Not Being A Tyrant
• People won't like me • It's a lonely place • Later I may need the support of someone I've been a Tyrant with • I don't want to be the bad guy	• I don't get to feel special • I don't get to feel powerful • I don't get to feel alive • If I'm not a Tyrant I'll be exploited or taken advantage of • I can't vent my anger; I'll have to control it

Desire To Be A Savior	Desire Not To Be A Savior
• It feels good • It feels like the right thing to do • I feel superior • I feel alive • My efforts count • I'm seen as a hero • I'm useful • People admire me • I have a purpose • People depend on me and need me	• I don't want people to depend on me • I feel ashamed of feeling superior • No good deed goes unpunished • I will become a target

Fear Of Being A Savior	Fear Of Not Being A Savior
• I encourage people to need me • People misunderstand me • I end up hurting the people I want to help • I'm not in my heart; I'm manipulating	• What will happen if I don't rescue? • I won't feel alive • I won't feel needed • I won't have a purpose • My efforts won't matter, and I won't matter

Desire To Be A Rebel	Desire Not To Be A Rebel
• I was born rebellious; I've been a Rebel all my life • It feels empowering • It feels liberating • I get to escape oppression • I get to feel superior • I get to act out my anger • I get to feel righteous • I am fighting for good causes • I feel special • I feel alive • Being a Rebel feels required to survive	• I just want to blend in • I get tired of fighting/ resisting • I'd like to resolve things rationally and not have to fight back • I want to be accepted regardless of what I believe

Fear Of Being A Rebel	Fear Of Not Being A Rebel
• I fear being disliked and becoming a target • I fear being punished • It's lonely • I want to be loved • I won't be seen for who I really am which is more than a Rebel • Some people will be jealous of me	• If I'm not a Rebel I'll be swallowed up—engulfed, destroyed • I'll be disempowered and exploited • The cause I'm fight for will be destroyed • Not being a Rebel feels weak • People are counting on me to lead the rebellion

END NOTES

[1] *Meeting The Shadow: The Hidden Power of The Dark Side Of Human Nature*, Edited by Connie Zweig and Jeremiah Abrams, Jeremy Tarcher/Putnam, 1991, p. 242

[2] Ibid, p. 243

[3] *Pathway to Bliss: Mythology and Personal Transformation*. Google Books, p. 123

[4] *The Shadow In America: Reclaiming The Soul Of A Nation*, Edited by Jeremiah Abrams, "Sacred Hunger," by Jacquelyn Small, p. 165.

[5] p. 78

[6] Robert Johnson, *Owning Your Own Shadow: Understanding The Dark Side of The Psyche*, Harper One, 1991, p.x

[7] Connie Zweig, Jeremiah Abrams, *Meeting The Shadow: The Hidden Power of the Dark Side of Human Nature*, Jeremy Tarcher, 1991, xxv

[8] Connie Zweig, Jeremiah Abrams, *Meeting The Shadow: The Hidden Power of the Dark Side of Human Nature*, Jeremy Tarcher, 1991, xxv

[9] "Essential Secrets Of Psychotherapy: What Is The Shadow?" Psychology Today, April 19, 2012 http://www.psychologytoday.com/blog/evil-deeds/201204/essential -secrets-psychotherapy-what-is-the-shadow

[10] "Former Ex-Gay Ministry Leader Comes Out, Recants Previous Teachings," Zack Ford, Think Progress, October 11, 2011, http:// thinkprogress.org/lgbt/2011/10/11/340335/former-ex-gay-ministry- leader-comes-out-recants-previous-teachings/

11 "Ex-Gay Leader Comes Out As Gay," Joe Morgan, Gay Star News, December 11, 2014, http://www.gaystarnews.com/article/ex-gay-leader- comes-out-gay111214#sthash.QhGlTuz6.dbf3

12 Carl Jung, transcript of "A Matter of The Heart," 1985, http://www.gnosis.org/gnostic-jung/Film-Transcript-Matter-of-Heart.html

13 *"Essential Secrets Of Psychotherapy: What Is The Shadow?" Psychology Today, April 19, 2012 http://www.psychologytoday.com/blog/evil-deeds/ 201204/essential-secrets-psychotherapy-what-is-the-shadow. [Should be cited as Ibid.*

14 Robert Bly, "The Long Bag We Drag Behind Us," from Meeting The Shadow: The Hidden Power Of The Dark Side of Human Nature, Jeremy Tarcher, Edited by Jeremiah Abrams and Connie Zwieg, 1991, p. 10

15 Ibid, p. 11

16 *Megge Fitz-Randolph, "The Collective Shadow In Jungian Psychology, https://suite.io/megge-hill-fitz-randolph/y692av*

17 Leslie Temple Thurston, *Marriage of Spirit: Enlightened Living In Today's World*, Corelight Publications, 2000, p. 20

18 *(Thurston 2000).*

19 Edward Whitmont, "The Evolution of The Shadow," *Meeting The Shadow: The Hidden Power Of The Dark Side of Human Nature*, Jeremy Tarcher, Edited by Jeremiah Abrams and Connie Zwieg, p. 17

20 D. Patrick Miller, "What The Shadow Knows: An Interview With John A. Sanford" in *Meeting The Shadow: The Hidden Power Of The Dark Side of Human Nature*, Jeremy Tarcher, Edited by Jeremiah Abrams and Connie Zwieg, p. 20

21 William Carl Eichman, "Meeting The Dark Side In Spiritual Practice," *Ibid.*, p. 134

22 Joseph Campbell, *The Power of Myth* (book), Anchor Publishing, 1991, Chapter 2

23 Joseph Campbell, *The Power of Myth* (book), Anchor Publishing, 1991, Chapter 2

24 *Andrew Harvey's* Light Upon Light*, Tarcher, 2004, p. 114*

25 Marketwatch, December 9, 2014, http://www.marketwatch. com/story/ two-psychologists-earned-81-million-from-cia-torture- program-2014-12-09

26 [Counterpunch, December 24, 2014, www.counterpunch.org/ 2014/12/24/weaponizing-psychology/]

27 [New York Times, December 14, 2014, www.nytimes.com/ 2014/12/15/opinion/charles-m-blow-america-who-are-we. html?_r=1]

28 "Obama: America 'Exceptional' So We Don't Prosecute Torturers," Common Dreams, December 10, 2014, http:// www.commondreams.org/ news/2014/12/10/obama-america-exceptional-so-we-dont-prosecute- torturers

29 [Eric Draitser, Russia TV Online, December 25, 2014, http:// rt.com/ op-edge/217575-police-violence-protests-usa/]

30 ["Noam Chomsky: 'Intentional Ignorance' Fuels American Racism" http:// www.salon.com/2015/03/18/ noam_chomsky_intentional_ ignorance_fuels_american_racism]

31 ["Psychology and Religion" (1938). In CW 11: Psychology and Religion: West and East. P.131]

32 [http://blacklivesmatter.com/a-herstory-of-the-blacklives matter- movement/]

33 [http://www.salon.com/2014/08/30/militarized_police_are _everywhere_when_police_officers_are_armed_an d_trained _like_soldiers_its_not_surprising_that_they_act_like_ soldiers/]

34 ["The Scapegoat Archetype," from The Shadow In America: Reclaiming The Soul Of A Nation, Edited by Jeramiah Abrams, Nataraj Publishing, 1994, p. 219]

35 [Ibid]

36 [Erich Neumann, Depth Psychology and A New Ethic, G.P. Putnam's Sons, 1969, p. 130]

37 [Jerome Bernstein, "An Archetypal Dilemma: The LA Riots," from The Shadow In America: Reclaiming The Soul Of A Nation, Edited by Jeramiah Abrams, Nataraj Publishing, 1994, p.241]

38 [Ibid]

39 [Ibid, p. 241-244]

40 [*Frederick Douglass Selected Speeches and Writings*]

41 [United States Military Casualties of War, http://en.wikipedia. org/ wiki/United_States_military_casualties_of_war]

42 [*Matthew Fox, The Hidden Spirituality Of Men: Ten Metaphors To Awaken The Sacred Masculine, New World Library, 2008, P. 78*]

43 [*"Like Wandering Ghosts," Ed Tick, Sun Magazine interview, June, 2008*]

44 [*Sun Magazine interview, 2008*]

45 [Ibid]

46 ["Women Who Risked Everything To Expose Sexual Assault In The Military," September 8, 2014, http://m.motherjones.com/ politics/ 2014/09/sexual-violence-american-military-photos]

47 *Huffington Post, November 8, 2011, http://www.huffingtonpost. com/ michael-meade-dhl/can-the-war-be-taken-out-_b_1077846. html*]

48 [War Is A Force That Gives Us Meaning, Anchor Paperback, 2003, P. 3]

49 [David Morris, *The Evil Hours: A Biography Of Post-Traumatic Stress Disorder,* Houghton-Mifflin, 2015, Introduction, P. 15]

50 [*"Troop Worship," Abby Martin, Counterpunch, January 7, 2015, http://www.counterpunch.org/2015/01/07/troop-worship/*]

51 ["Can The War Be Taken Out Of Warriors?" Huffington Post, November 8, 2011, http://www.huffingtonpost.com/michael-meade-dhl/ can-the-war-be-taken-out-_b_1077846.html]

52 [Evil Hours, p. 159]

53 Ibid.

54 [*The Evil Hours, p.251*]

55 http://www.theatlantic.com/features/archive/2014/12/ the-tragedy-of- the-american-military/383516/]

56 [http://www.carolynbaker.net/2013/03/19/creating-the-new-story-the- masculine-and-the-feminine-by-gary-stamper/]

57 [*"What A Destructive Wall St. Owes Young Americans," Ralph Nader, The Nader Page, March 14, 2014, https://blog.nader. org/2014/03/14/destructive- wall-street-owes-young-americans/*]

58 ["Ronald Reagan, Mental Health, and Spin," MI Watch, 2011, http:// www.miwatch.org/2011/02/ ronald reagan and mental.html]

59 [Tom Brown website]

60 *[Carolyn Baker, Guy McPherson, Extinction Dialogs: How To Live With Death In Mind, Tayen Lane Publishing, Oakland, 2014, Foreword]*

61 *["The Planetary Hospice Movement," by Zhiwa Woodbury, 2014, http:// www.planetary-hospice.com/wp-content/uploads/2014/10/ Principles-of- Planetary-Hospice.pdf]*

62 [Ibid]

63 *[Baker, McPherson, Extinction Dialogs: How To Live With Death In Mind, Foreword]*

64 [h#p://ronyabanks.com/2011/11/27/death—dying—a— buddhist— perspective/]

65 "People Would Rather Be Electrically Shocked Than Left Alone With Their Thoughts," by Nadia Whitehead, Science Magazine, July 3, 2014, http://news.sciencemag.org/brain-behavior/2014/07/people-would- rather-be-electrically-shocked-left-alone-their-thoughts]

66 *["Study Links Selfies To Narcissism And Psychopathy," by Carolyn Gregoire, Huffington Post, January 12, 2015, http://www. huffingtonpost.com/ 2015/01/12/selfies-narcissism-psychopathy n 6429358.html? utm hp ref=mostpopular]*

67 [United Nations Resource for Speakers on Global Issues, http:// www.un.org/en/globalissues/briefingpapers/food/vitalstats. shtml]

68 *["The Power and The Glory: They Myth of American Exceptionalism," Howard Zinn, Boston Review, June 1, 2005, http://bostonreview. net/zinn- power-glory]*

69 ["Six Habits Of Highly Empathic People," Greater Good website, November 27, 2012, www.greatergood.berkeley.edu/ article/item/ six habits of highly empathic people1]

70 ["Six Habits Of Highly Empathic People," Greater Good website, November 27, 2012, http://greatergood.berkeley.edu/ article/item/ six habits of highly empathic people1]

71 [Gabor Mate, *In The Realm of The Hungry Ghosts*, North Atlantic Books, 2010.]

72 [Francis Weller—"The Reverence of Approach," April 1, 2015 http:// www.enteringthehealingground.com/trail-notes/the-reverence-of- approach]

73 [Mark Nepo, The Endless Practice: Becoming Who You Were Born To Be, Atria Books, 2014, p. 150]

74 [David Stendl-Rast, *Gratefulness The Heart of Prayer: An Approach To Life In Fullness,* Paulist Press, 1984, P. 15]

75 [*Ibid*]

76 [Derrick Jensen, Endgame, Vol I, Seven Stories Press, 2006, p. 332.]

77 [Zen Peacemakers, *http://zenpeacemakers.org/bernie-glassman/*]

78 [Foreword, Carolyn Baker and Guy McPherson: Extinction Dialogs: How To Live With Death In Mind, Tayen Lane Publishing, 2014, P.16]

79 Ibid.

80 ["Activism In The New Story," Charles Eisenstein, The New And Ancient Story website, http://www.thenewandancientstory. net/home/ activism-in-the-new-story]

81 [Francis Weller, Entering The Healing Ground: Grief, Ritual, and The Soul of The World, Wisdom Bridge Press, 2011, PP 83-84]

82 [Ann Amberg Masters Thesis, http://lorianassociation.com/master- theses/]

83 ["What Is Action?" Charles Eisenstein, January 30, 2015, http:// www.thenewandancientstory.net/home/what-is-action]

84 ["The Wounded Healer, Part 2", Paul Levy, Awaken In The Dream, 2010, http://www.awakeninthedream.com/wordpress/the-wounded-healer-part-2/]

85 [Goodreads quote: https://www.goodreads.com/quotes/751027-i-love- because-my-love-is-not-dependent-on-the]

86 ["What Is Action?" by Charles Eisenstein, January 30, 2015, www.thenewandancientstory.net/home/what-is-action]

87 [Mark Nepo, Endless Practice: Becoming Who You Were Born To Be, Atria Books, 2014, pp. 232-233.]

88 [Barbara Brown Taylor, "In Praise of Darkness", Time, April 17, 2014, www.time.com/65543/barbara-brown-taylor-in-praise-of-darkness/]

89 *[Barbara Brown Taylor, "In Praise of Darkness", Time, April 17, 2014, http://time.com/65543/barbara-brown-taylor-in-praise-of-darkness/]*

90 [https://www.youtube.com/watch?v=93EqVQuTJ-o]

91 *[http://michaeldev.bigrigmedia.com/app/uploads/2015/02/A-Marion-   Woodman-Perspective-on-the-Embodied-Psyche-Experiential- Integration-.pdf]*

92 ["Spiritual Bypassing, Relationship, and The Dharma," by John Welwood at the Jill Edwards Minye website, www.jillminye.com/#!human-nature-buddha-nature-by/cfnz]

93 ["Spiritual Bypassing: Avoidance In Holy Drag," by Robert Augustus Masters, http://robertmasters.com/writings/spiritual-bypassing/]

94 *[Carl Jung, Psychology and Religion, Yale University Press, 1960, page number unknown]*

95 [Bernie Glassman, Zen Peacemakers website, www.zenpeacemakers.org/bernie-glassman/]

96 ["Stone Pillow," Wikipedia, http://en.wikipedia.org/wiki/ Stone Pillow]

97 [http://www.corelight.org/store/index.php/audio/talks-on-special- topics/for-love-and-money-recorded-in-portland.html]

98 *[Barbara Ehrenreich, Bright-Sided: How the Relentless Promotion of Positive Thinking Has Undermined America]*

99 [Debbie Ford, Riverhead Books, 2010, pp 39-54]

100 ["Shadow Projection: The Fuel Of War, Paul Levy, 2010, www.awakeninthedream.com/wordpress/shadow-projection-the-fuel- of-war/]

101 [Collected Works of C.G. Jung, Volume 14: Mysterium Coniunctionis, p. 365]

102 *["Shadow Projection: The Fuel Of War, Paul Levy, 2010, http://www.awakeninthedream.com/wordpress/shadow-projection-the-fuel-of- war/]*

103   *[IMBd Movie Synopsis website: http://www.imdb.com/title/ tt0091530/ synopsis]*

104   [pp.125-126]

105   ["The Ego and Its Projections, Jenna Lilla, Path of Soul website, http://pathofsoul.org/2013/01/22/the-ego-and-its-projections/]

106   [*Owning Your Shadow: Understanding The Dark Side of The Psyche*, Harper Collins, 1993, p. 27]

107   Ibid

108   —*Out Of Weakness: Healing The Wounds That Drive Us To War, Andrew Bard Schmookler*

Printed in the United States
By Bookmasters